> type <

veruschka götz

> type <

for the internet

and other

digital media

ava

®

AVA Publishing SA
Switzerland

Sterling Publishing Co., Inc.
New York

An AVA Book
Published by AVA Publishing SA
Rue du Bugnon 7
CH-1299 Crans-près-Céligny
Switzerland
Tel: +41 786 005 109
Email: enquiries@avabooks.ch

Distributed by Thames and Hudson
(ex-North America)
181a High Holborn
London WC1V 7QX
United Kingdom
Tel: +44 20 7845 5000
Fax: +44 20 7845 5055
Email: sales@thameshudson.co.uk
www.thamesandhudson.com

Distributed by Sterling Publishing Co., Inc.
in USA
387 Park Avenue South
New York, NY 10016-8810
Tel: +1 212 532 7160
Fax: +1 212 213 2495
www.sterlingpub.com

in Canada
Sterling Publishing
c/o Canadian Manda Group
One Atlantic Avenue, Suite 105
Toronto, Ontario M6K 3E7

English Language Support Office
AVA Publishing (UK) Ltd.
Tel: +44 1903 204 455
Email: enquiries@avabooks.co.uk

ISBN 2-88479-002-0

10 9 8 7 6 5 4 3 2 1

Design by Veruschka Götz

English translation by Jörg von Stein, Berlin,
Richard Holmes, Berlin and David Wilby, Berlin

Production and separations
by AVA Book Production Pte. Ltd., Singapore
Tel: +65 6334 8173
Fax: +65 6334 0752
Email: production@avabooks.com.sg

veruschka götz

> type <

for the **internet**

and other
digital media

content

008.009

»The image of the man on strike [...],
staring at a blank screen will one day
be seen as one of the most beautiful pictures
of 20th-century anthropology.«
Jean Baudrillard

Anarchy in the virtual realm

It wasn´t so very long ago that the term »anarchy« struck terror into the soul of the middle classes: fantasies abounded of a society without control, and of law and order, political authority and accepted structures being swept away. Today in the Internet age the term »anarchy« takes on a different meaning, radiating an aura of something positive, that which is desired. The Internet, a grass-roots evolution, a podium for free speech and an engine of democracy, stands opposed to existing hierarchies. It is against centralisation, capital, authority, structures and any game plan order.

If authority is abandoned then the stage is set for the illusion of self-control to take over, which aspires to no particular goal. This rejection of the rules not only spawns a mass of information lacking any specific aims, but also intolerable lawlessness in terms of the way the information is supplied and its aesthetic quality. Paradoxically, instead of enjoying a freedom newly won, we experience the very lack of it, because the way the information is coded is a many-layered maze in the middle of which the recipient becomes lost.

Over-ambitious screen designers intent on showing off their design skills blindly adapt the printer´s rulebook to the screen and worse, manifest an ignorance only equalled by their confidence in having developed an especially outstanding graphic interface. Without an editor or anyone to police the aesthetics, both the sender and the receiver come to grief. Neither has control over the information supplied. Instead the recipient becomes bogged down in a mire of data and information as a result of all this freedom. Such lawlessness engenders lawlessness of the typographical kind: freedom at the expense of aesthetics. The screen is an independent medium and must be understood and put to use as such.

A good interface should permit the user to establish a quick and clear overview of the contents being shown and allow easy navigation through the available data with no loss of direction.

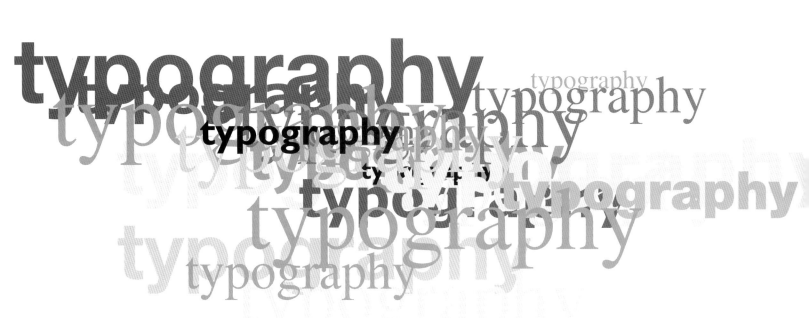

For technical reasons, the appearance of text on the screen is not of the same quality as it would be in print media. Reading from the screen is far more strenuous for the eyes than reading from paper, and screen designers should take this into account. Typography for the screen demands that we as designers observe different rules. Print-based design rules cannot simply be transferred to the screen and the screen cannot be treated as though it were paper.

Featuring numerous examples of screen-based type usage »Type for the Internet and Other Digital Media« describes how attributes are modified in relationship to type size, type designs, colour and contrast. Furthermore the book examines and compares various typeface classifications such as serifs, sans serifs and computer typefaces, and considers their effectiveness on screen. Also examined in the book is how to build up identities with digital media and how to transfer existing identities on to the Internet without jeopardising an already established corporate image.

The aim of this book is to show the reader how to achieve optimum legibility and clarity in screen-based typography usage, and in doing so, supply content and graphics in different ways to print-based tradition. Both the advantages and disadvantages of typographical design on screen are shown.

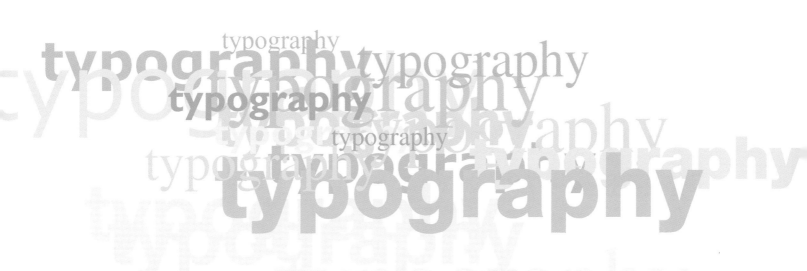

excerpts
012.013

Suitability

Chapter 2, 5

Serif fonts are very good when text is printed on paper. But on the screen sans serif fonts are better, because without as many fine lines they are clearer and create fewer pixel effects. Some fonts are harder to read on screen and will make the reader tire quickly.

Chapter 2, 5

Texts on screen set in grotesque typefaces work very well on the screen as large and bold types.

Chapter 2

The aim of text design is to make the text as easy to read as possible. The type size is a very important parameter influencing good legibility. Type sizes that can be read on paper, i.e. **9 pt**, without any problems may be illegible on screen because of the poor resolution.

Chapter 1, 2

In order to produce a uniform overall appearance, it is important to avoid using more type sizes than is necessary.

Chapter 2

All the options available to make text easier to read on screen – larger font size, more spacing between characters, interlinear spacing – **have the disadvantage that the final text needs more space than the comparable text printed on paper. Texts on screen should therefore be kept as short as possible to avoid unnecessary scrolling.**

Chapter 2

Although the landscape format of the screen makes it very tempting to use long lines of text, it is important that the lines should be kept short.

Chapter 2

The length of lines has to be matched to the spacing between the lines: The longer the lines then the greater the space needed between them.

Chapter 2

The letter spacing for text on screen should be wider by five to ten units. That especially applies to bold styles, because otherwise the letters may run together or merge in small sizes, which means that letters may be misread.

Chapter 5

The maxim for suitable types for screen must be: bigger, wider, further.

Colours

Chapter 2, 4

As a mode of emphasis, colour tends to work very well: colour changes, if made in a screen-friendly font, produce clear highlighting that is better than, say, small caps, italics or underlining. By adjusting the strength of the colour contrast, the intensity of the highlight can be determined. Care must still be taken to ensure that the colour used for emphasis forms an acceptable contrast with the background, as indeed should the main text.

Chapter 2

A typeface which is harmonised with the background makes the text easy to read. If the colour is too glaring or the contrast is too great then the overall impression can be fuzzy, and the text is difficult to read.
Intensive contrasts, e.g. complementary colour contrasts, are very well suited to attracting attention, say on a home page. It is this same intensity, though, that makes them unsuitable as main themes.

Additional leading **between lines up to about 150% of the compressed typeface size can improve legibility on screen considerably.**

For text that might have to be edited quickly and have a font size of less than 10 pt, anti-aliasing **should not be used.**

It does not necessarily always follow that anti-aliasing **improves readability: with some typefaces (bitmaps) and smaller texts, it is better not to use smooth finishing.**

Information is provided piece by piece, **so that the reader finds it easier to absorb the message, despite the poor screen resolution.**

For text that has to be edited quickly **and small typefaces, it is better to use a well designed screen font.**

When designing information on screen, ease of navigation and orientation are just as important as the choice of easy-to-read fonts.

Transferring type from print to screen: Using typographical »quotations« **the overall impression and recognition value is maintained.**

With digital media, the visual sensation **is often more important than the transport of information. If it is necessary for a text to be easily read then the designer must take more care when presenting it than would be necessary on paper, because of the limitations of screen resolution.**

Attributes that can make text easier to read on screen when used appropriately are:
The choice of type
The choice of type size
Tracking
Line length
Interlinear spacing

The main horizontal and vertical strokes **of a font should, ideally, align perfectly with the pixel grid. If the strokes are thinner than one pixel, which they obviously can't be, so the characters vary.**

When choosing a typeface for the screen it is advisable to pay attention to the x-height: **the more generous this is then the easier it will be to read the final product.**

Black backgrounds **promote readability on screen. Black on the screen means that there is no light being emitted. This reduces the chances of flicker-effect.**

The colour resolution for anti-aliasing should neither be too high nor too deep: Too few colours can mean that those used for the text don't combine well with the background, while too many colours will increase the file size of the graphic image. An acceptable representation taking up relatively little memory space is a resolution of 256 colours.

The choice of type size depends among other things on the nature of the background. If it is unsettled or there is little contrast **between background and typeface then it is advisable to use a larger font.**

The readability of a text is not only affected by the defining factors of typeface and type size, but also of colour contrast **between the text and the background.**

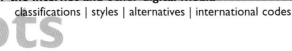

excerpts 014.015

Classifications

Chapter 2, 3, 5

Usually fonts for the screen are designed as sans serifs, with large x-heights, and generous widths. Pixel fonts for short words as used in buttons, usually consist of capital letters only for better reproduction in small sizes.

Chapter 2, 5

The neo grotesque Lineales types show up very well on screen.

Chapter 5

Not all sans serifs work on screen. The Humanist and Geometric varieties should be carefully assessed in advance of their planned application.

Chapter 2, 5

Although very effective on paper, serif typefaces only look good on screen when they are very large.

Chapter 5

Slab serifs with their good legibility on screen provide a good alternative to Antiqua fonts.

Styles

Chapter 2

Italic and compressed styles are not really suitable as modes of emphasis for the screen.
As an alternative, variations in text colour may be used or, where a subtler effect is required, the text colour simply applied at a reduced tone.

Chapter 2

Extreme type styles such as condensed, in particular, ultracondensed as well as very bold ought not to be used on the screen: they can often only be presented in a distorted form (condensed) or tend to clump together (bold). Factors influencing this are type size and the colour contrast of the text to background.

Chapter 2

Unwanted ligatures – when letters seem tied together – can result if a very small typeface size is used, or a bold font design.
In such cases, letter spacing should be added.

Alternatives

Chapter 3

The Internet is a global network. In order to overcome language barriers to its international application, visual markers, pictograms and icons have become important alternatives to text.

Chapter 3

As long as the screen continues to rely on today's poor standards of resolution, it is appropriate that design for the medium be based more around pictorial information than detailed reams of text.

Chapter 3

The degree to which an icon's meaning is immediately clear depends to a large extent on whether it is modelled on a well-known metaphor.

Chapter 3

The range of possibilities afforded by new media is still not fully applied. Try voice or visual animation instead of poorly displayed text.

With their intricacy and rich, curvilinear detail Arabic and Indian fonts have to be very carefully considered as to their suitability on screen.

Used on the screen, script styles and experimental fonts can make reading awkward. Their suitability should be checked carefully in each case but it may be better to leave them out since there is a large margin for error. Modes of emphasis, such as colour, work well while underlining is best left out – again decisions have to be made according to the situation.

Computer fonts provide solutions to problems of screen display. Even in small sizes (e.g. 10 pt) they still read well, which conventional type cannot achieve.

Screen fonts have been devised specifically for screen applications. Often they look crude on paper.

Because of their complexity Chinese and Japanese scripts are difficult to display on screen. They need to be used large, in order not to appear untidy, cluttered, or lumped.
The structured appearance of Korean script makes it almost ideal for on screen adaptation.

Cyrillic, Greek, and Hebrew scripts are linked by strong geometry, a common sense of proportion, and a constructed effect, which makes them easy to adapt for on-screen use.

The various forms of emphasis can be used to produce a semiotic expression of a word.

Various font sizes and styles should be tested before a font is used for screen text presentations. It is not always the case that the larger the font size then the easier it will be to read.

Traditional typography has a large number of options that either don't function on the screen at all, or only do so to a limited extent. Included among these are italics and finer styles, which should where possible be avoided.

international codes

All terms should be easily understood by Internet users all over the world. But not only the terms differ, care must also be taken with the use of colours, because their connotations can also differ widely from culture to culture.

Colours can have a different significance in different countries and societies. In worldwide communications, for example with the Internet, this culture-specific interpretation of colour represents a real challenge for designers.

016.017

What are the differences between type families?
What belongs to a type family?
What are appropriate proportions, spacings and
layouts for good legibility?

Type families

The designer can already determine the effect created by a publication with the choice between a serif or sans serif font. This choice influences texts with regard to the aesthetic, formal, functional and psychological aspects.

»Exhaustion is the quickest way to equality and fraternity,
and the liberty
is finally added by sleep.«
Friedrich Nietzsche

Helvetica
Lineales

Times

Georgia
Transitionals

Bembo
Antiqua

Transitionals
Transitional Times, which is generally a fairly condensed typeface, was designed in 1923 by Stanley Morison for the newspaper of the same name, »The Times«. It was specially developed for newspaper printing, which requires good legibility on lower-quality paper.

News gothic
Lineales

Bodoni
Didones (Modern Face)

Futura
Lineales

Frutiger
Lineales

Garamond
Humanists and Garaldes

Walbaum
Humanists and Garaldes

Rotis Sans Serif

Rockwell
Lineales

Lineales

Typeface families

In present-day usage we distinguish between two main typeface groups. These are old-style typefaces (serifs) and gothic typefaces (sans serifs). In old-style typefaces, the characters have fine terminal strokes, known as serifs. This group includes the classifications Humanists and Garaldes (for example, Garamond, Goudy, Palatino or Sabon), Transitionals (for example, Baskerville, Caslon, Century Schoolbook, Concorde, Poppl Pontifex, Times or ITC Cheltenham) and Didones or Modern Faces (for example, Madison, Bodoni or Walbaum).

The stroke weights of these typefaces with serifs differ considerably, making them ideal for use as body text in books and newspapers due to their good legibility.

Sans serifs, also known as Lineales, do not have the terminal strokes of the serif typefaces. The stroke weights of these typefaces differ only slightly or not at all and are used mainly for titles, headlines, on posters, in advertising and as body texts, such as this one, which has been set in Gill Sans.

Another typeface group is the slab serifs, also known as Egyptiennes. These typefaces have more or less emphasised serifs. They are mainly used for display work and headlines.

The rules which apply to the sans serifs also apply to the serif typefaces. The typeface family should be chosen with great care, since the typeface used has a crucial influence on the text with regard to the aesthetic, formal, functional and psychological aspects.

Legibility can also be a significant criterion when selecting a typeface. Each family, for example Univers, is made up of a variety of different type designs, such as light, regular, medium, bold, condensed and extended, in addition to italics – providing a huge amount of freedom in the overall design. Extreme designs, such as extra condensed, are difficult to read and should only be used in special cases.

Serif fonts are very good when text is printed on paper. But on the screen sans serif fonts are better, because without as many fine lines they are clearer and create fewer pixel effects. Some fonts are harder to read on screen and will make the reader tire quickly.

grids **times**

Visual and functiona
continuity in the org
screen design, grap
design, and typogra
are impor when it cc
to convincing the re

It wasn't so very lc
the term »anarchy«
into the soul of the
middle classes:
fantasies were abou

Akzidenz grotesk

Lineales

Gill Sans

Lineales

Clarendon

Slab Serifs
The Clarendon typeface was developed in England in about 1845. Originally designed for lexical applications, it has been used as a typewriter font, for advertising, and in newspapers. Classical Roman typefaces such as Bookman and Bodoni were the models for Clarendon.

Trixie Text

Lineales

Formata

Lineales

Avant garde

Lineales

Palatino

Humanists and Garaldes

Stone Sans

Lineales

Century Gothic

Lineales

Avenir

Lineales

Stone Serif

Humanists and Garaldes

Univers

Lineales
Univers was designed in 1957 by Adrian Frutiger. It met with a very warm reception because it was produced in systematically numbered typeface cuts. To this day it is one of the most popular grotesque typefaces.

Meta Plus

Lineales

Aa **Fraktur**
Black letter, also known as broken type, is a very old type style (dating back to approx. 1163). The characters stand upright and are sharply slanted at the ends. This typeface is hardly used nowadays since a lot of people find it difficult to read. Some newspapers use this kind of typeface for their title, since it gives the impression of seriousness and permanence. The Frankfurter Allgemeine Zeitung is one example.

Aa **Roman typefaces**
The Roman typefaces (known in Germany as Antiqua) are based on ancient Greek and Roman manuscripts that were rediscovered in the Renaissance. The characters used have changed little to this day – though there have been stylistic adaptations. The Roman typefaces are characterised by serifs and differing line strengths.

Aa **Slab Serifs**
In the 18th century the Roman typefaces gave rise to Linear antiqua. This group has serifs that are more or less emphasised. The differences in line thickness are not as pronounced as in its predecessors, or they have completely disappeared. These typefaces were once used to highlight text. After the Second World War they became very popular with German and Swiss graphic designers.

Aa **Lineales**
This group has no serifs. Around the beginning of the 20th century, the development of this typeface had advanced to a stage at which it could be used as the basic typeface for major publications. A milestone was the appearance of the Akzidenz grotesk around 1900. With its anonymous, sober and modern appearance, this was one of the most frequently used typefaces until the 1960s. The sans serif Linear antiqua has an ageless elegance.

Font sizes

The aim of text design is to make the text as easy
to read as possible. The type size is a very important
parameter influencing good legibility.

»Every sign on its own seems dead.
What gives it life? It lives in use.
Does it have the breath of life within itself?
Or is the use its breath?«
Ludwig Wittgenstein

DTP point | pt
0.352 mm
0.0139 in (1:72)

Didot point | dd
0.376 mm

Cicero | cc
4.5 mm
12 dd

Millimetre | mm
2.83 pt
2.67 dd

Inch | in
25.4 mm
72 pt

Extra large | 18 point and larger   Headings | Overhead foils

this size can be used f

48 point

this size can be used for he

36 point

this size can be used for headings

24 point

Standard | 8–12 point   Basic text | Reading text

12 **point**

11 **point**

10 **point**

9 point

8 point

Font sizes   The aim of text design is not just to produce
an overall impression that is pleasing to the
eye, but also a text that is as easy to read as
possible. Good readability depends on the right
combination of various parameters such as
typeface, type size, character and line spacing,
text formatting and alignment.

The type size is important because this influences
a number of other parameters such as column
width, line spacing, and so on. Over the long
history of typography various measuring systems
have been developed, in much the same way as
distances are measured in miles or kilometres.
Most computer programs make use of the DTP
point, so that this has become a widely accepted
international measure.

On the basis of the type size for the basic text it
is possible to derive all the other quantities. The
choice of the type size for the body of the text
will depend on the format, the amount of text to
be included, and the nature of the publication:
advertising copy requires a larger type size than
a text book. For most purposes, the type size
should be between 9 and 12 point. The heading
that »lures« the reader into the text will normally
be larger – between 12 and 18 point. For marginal
notes and footnotes, a size of 6 to 8 point is
appropriate. In this way the text is clearly
organised with a hierarchical structure.

Type sizes that can be read on paper without any problems may be illegible on screen because of poor resolution.

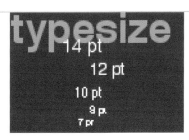

typesize

14 pt

12 pt

10 pt

9 p.

7 pt

Large | 12–18 point   Headings | Overhead foils | Text on screen

this size can be used for texts on screen
18 point

this size can be used for texts on screen
16 point

this size can be used for texts on screen
14 point

The closer the text sizes of the various levels are together then the more elegant the overall impression. However, there should be a difference of at least two points.
As an alternative, instead of using different text sizes it is possible to set higher level texts such as headings in the same type size as the body of the text, but with a bolder typeface.

Consultation sizes | 6–8 point
Marginal notes | Footnotes | Small amounts of text

this size can be used for small amounts of text
8 point

7 point

6 point

The classical style format

Heading | 24 pt

Subheading | 18 pt

Intermediate headings | 12 pt

Basic text | 9–10 pt

In order to produce a uniform overall appearance, it is important to avoid using more different type sizes than is necessary.

Combinations of type sizes
Heading | Body of text | Marginal notes

This is a headline in 14 pt

A suitable type size is 9 point. The type sizes should differ by at least two points between the levels.

A footnote is subordinate to the main body of text, and this is reflected in the very small type size, such as the 6 point used here.

This is a headline in 9 pt

If the heading has the same type size as the rest of the text then it should be set in a bold or italic face to make the difference clear.

A footnote is subordinate to the main body of text, and this is reflected in the very small type size, such as the 7 point used here.

This is a headline in 16 pt
The subheading is in 12 pt

A suitable type size is 10 point. The type sizes should differ by at least two points between the levels.

A footnote is subordinate to the main body of text, and this is reflected in the very small type size, such as the 8 point used here.

I.03

Typeface fonts | forms of emphasis

Not all type styles are suitable for use as emphasis.
In particular italics and small and thin styles have to
be set against a suitable background.
The designer should also take into account the
semiotic expression each emphasis can evoke.

»Font asceticism and restriction of the variety
is what is really necessary.«
Otl Aicher

old Avantgarde   new Bodoni   **light** Helvetica Black   heavy **Helvetica Ultra Light**

**The various forms of
emphasis can be used
to produce a semiotic
expression of a word.**

light   normal   **semi-bold**   **bold**   *italic*   condensed   extended

<u>underline</u>   w i d e   s p a c i n g   **Type**face   Type size   Grotesque | Antiqu

SMALL CAPS   Outlining   UPPER CASE   Colour   **background**

Positioning

Typeface fonts and forms of emphasis		
Typeface fonts and forms of emphasis	One way of drawing attention to headings, text passages or specific words is to use different type sizes. However, this should be used sparingly, because there is a risk the overall impression can be impaired.	It is possible to distinguish between: **Aesthetic emphasis** This fits into the overall optical image e.g. a text in italics.

**Typeface fonts and forms
of emphasis**

One way of drawing attention to headings, text
passages or specific words is to use different
type sizes. However, this should be used sparingly,
because there is a risk the overall impression can
be impaired.

In order to structure texts or to highlight parts
of a text it is also possible to use the same size
typeface, but different weights. A member of a
type family is defined first by the name, then the
weight and shape, such as Bodoni, semi-bold,
condensed, italic.

Other design features such as underlining, wide-
spacing, switching between grotesque and antiqua
etc. can be used to emphasise special features of
a text. However, the various forms of emphasis
should be used with care: only where it is
functional and necessary.

It is possible to distinguish between:
Aesthetic emphasis
This fits into the overall optical image
e.g. a text in italics.
Optical emphasis
This stands out against the body of text
e.g. bold text.
Inverse emphasis
A background can change the appearance of a
text dramatically. But it is important that it is
not used with light weights of a typeface, as
these can merge with the background on
printing.

Ultra Light and light styles are not suitable for the screen because the lines are too thin for the pixels unless the type is used in very large type sizes. Italic styles and narrow letter spacing should also be avoided. With bold type, the lines should not be too thick because this could make the letters run together.

Helvetica
Helvetica
Helvetica
Helvetica
Helvetica
Helvetica
Helvetica

The designation of type-faces can vary considerably depending on the producer. In order to achieve uniform designations, a standard numbering system is some-times used. This is the case, for example with Univers and Helvetica.

		extra extended	extended	extended italic	normal	normal italic	condensed	condensed italic	extra condensed
		_2	_3	_4	_5	_6	_7	_8	_9
ultra light	2_		ma	ma	ma	ma	ma	ma	
thin	3_		ma	ma	ma	ma	ma	ma	
light	4_		ma	ma	ma	ma	ma	ma	
normal	5_		ma	ma	ma	ma	ma	ma	
medium	6_		ma	ma	ma	ma	ma	ma	
bold	7_		ma	ma	ma	ma	ma	ma	
heavy	8_		ma	ma	ma	ma	ma	ma	
black	9_		ma	ma	ma	ma	ma	ma	

The Helvetica Type family
The first digit denotes the weight (2x–9x), where five (5x) is the normal type weight. The second digit (x3–x9) provides further information about the shape, where again the five (x5) is the normal value.

Examples
normal Helvetica is: Helvetica 55
medium italic Helvetica is: Helvetica 66
bold, extended italic Helvetica is: Helvetica 74

2
Helvetica 23 Ultra Light Extended
Helvetica 24 Ultra Light Extended Italic
Helvetica 25 Ultra Light
Helvetica 26 Ultra Light Italic
Helvetica 27 Ultra Light Condensed
Helvetica 28 Ultra Light Condensed Italic

3
Helvetica 33 Thin Extended
Helvetica 34 Thin Extended Italic
Helvetica 35 Thin
Helvetica 36 Thin Italic
Helvetica 37 Thin Condensed
Helvetica 38 Thin Condensed Italic

4
Helvetica 43 Light Extended
Helvetica 44 Light Extended Italic
Helvetica 45 Light
Helvetica 46 Light Italic
Helvetica 47 Light Condensed
Helvetica 48 Light Condensed Italic

5
Helvetica 53 Extended
Helvetica 54 Extended Italic
Helvetica 55 Normal
Helvetica 56 Normal Italic
Helvetica 57 Condensed
Helvetica 58 Condensed Italic

6
Helvetica 63 Medium Extended
Helvetica 64 Medium Extended Italic
Helvetica 65 Medium
Helvetica 66 Medium Italic
Helvetica 67 Medium Condensed
Helvetica 68 Medium Condensed Italic

7
Helvetica 73 Bold Extended
Helvetica 74 Bold Extended Italic
Helvetica 75 Bold
Helvetica 76 Bold Italic
Helvetica 77 Bold Condensed
Helvetica 78 Bold Condensed Italic

8
Helvetica 83 Heavy Extended
Helvetica 84 Heavy Extended Italic
Helvetica 85 Heavy
Helvetica 86 Heavy Italic
Helvetica 87 Heavy Condensed
Helvetica 88 Heavy Condensed Italic

9
Helvetica 93 Black Extended
Helvetica 94 Black Extended Italic
Helvetica 95 Black
Helvetica 96 Black Italic
Helvetica 97 Black Condensed
Helvetica 98 Black Condensed Italic

I.04

The choice of spacing between words and characters determines whether the overall impression (colour) of a text is harmonious and the text is easy to read.

»...the design of fonts is all about
bringing the black and white into the right balance.
Otl Aicher

In order to produce a text that is pleasant to read it is important to have an even colour, i.e. to avoid dark areas where words are fitted closely together, and »holes« where words are more widely spaced. This is a problem with justified texts when the words are pushed together or pulled apart to make them fit on the line.

The word spacing is linked to the letter spacing
Helvetica 14 pt

The word spacing is linked to the letter spacing
Helvetica Light 14 pt

The word spacing is linked to the letter spacing
Helvetica Condensed 14 pt

The word spacing is linked to the letter spacing
Helvetica Medium Extended 14 pt

The word spacing is linked to the letter spacing
Avantgarde 14 pt

The word spacing is linked to the letter spacing
Times 14 pt

Spacing and punch widths

In order to produce a text that is pleasant to read it is important to avoid dark areas where words are fitted closely together and »holes« where words are further apart. This is a problem with justified texts when the words are pushed together or pulled apart to make them fit on the line. The lower case »i« set between the words is used as a measure.

The spacing between the words is related to the space between letters and the punch width (the inner spaces of the letters). If the letter spacing is increased then the word spacing must also be increased so that the word can still be readily identified as a unit.

a
Avantgarde

a
Courier

typography
Helvetica 35

typography
Helvetica 53

typography
Helvetica 57

The letter spacing for texts on the screen should be wider by five to ten units. That especially applies to bold styles, because otherwise the letters may run together or merge in small sizes, which means that letters may be misread.

typography
Helvetica 55

typography
Helvetica 95

typography
Helvetica 55 + 5

typography
Helvetica 95 +10

Thick and light fonts should be set with larger word spacing and letter spacing, because of the large inner spaces of the letters (punch width).

Theiwordispacingiisidefinedibyitheiwidthiofitheilowericaseii.

Thin and bold fonts can be set with letters and words closer together because the inner spaces of the letters (punch widths) are smaller.

Depending on the type case and weight the punch width can vary.

Punch width

a   a   a   a   a   a
Futura   Garamond   Gill Sans Impact   Times   Verdana

a   a   a   a   a   a
35 Helvetica Thin   55 Helvetica   63 Helvetica   65 Helvetica   67 Helvetica   95 Helvetica
                                   Medium Extended   Medium   Medium Condensed   Black

1.05

Not every typeface can be used for all purposes.
Before a designer chooses a form of alignment, it
is necessary to determine the aim of a publication.

»Looking at our letters set together in a way
that is unusual to us offends the eye and
takes the expression out of the words.«
Mark Twain

When checking letter
spacing it can help if you
turn the word upside down
or look at the reverse
image.

Upper case letters that produce open spacing.

A L T V W

Lower case letters that produce open spacing.

f r v w y   e o a

Particularly if these letters occur in pairs,
kerning is necessary for large font sizes.

Space before **A**   Space after **V   H**

Tea   VAULT   ⊥ꓥ∩Aꓥ

Letter spacing

Software fonts for computers are usually
accompanied with a kerning table that adjusts
the spaces on either side of a letter to produce
results that are generally acceptable for all but
the largest font sizes. Kerning longer texts letter
by letter is extremely time-consuming, and this
is only practical for headings or individual words
on posters.

When deciding whether additional kerning is
necessary, look at the spacing between a pair
of letters. Overuse of kerning can also be a
problem if letters are placed so close together
that they can no longer be separated by
the reader.

With digital media, the visual sensation is often more important than the transport of information.
If it is necessary for a text to be easily read then the designer must take more care when presenting it than would be necessary on paper, because of the limitations of screen resolution.

The length of the line and the font size should fit together so that the resultant text is easy to read. The longer a text column is the more opportunities there are to produce a smooth overall impression.

Tracking – when letter spacing is increased over a line, or more than a line – can be used in order to avoid »holes« in justified text. Word spacing can also be increased or words can be hyphenated. With narrow columns it is better to set a right ragged text.

This text is aligned down the left margin and is right ragged. Left aligned texts must be set with a font size that is suitable for the line width, because otherwise there can easily be large holes at the end of the lines, giving the text an unsettled appearance.

This text is justified. The beginning and end of every line is aligned. This is achieved by varying the spacing between words and between letters. The disadvantage is that it can lead to uneven colour, with »holes«, particularly if the column is not wide enough for the font size being used. Newspaper and book texts are generally justified.

This text is justified. The beginning and end of every line is aligned. This is achieved by varying the spacing between words and between letters. The disadvantage is that it can lead to uneven colour, with »holes«, particularly if the column is not wide enough for the font size being used. Newspaper and book texts are generally justified.

This text is centrally aligned.
The alignment is around the middle axis,
and there is no alignment of text at the beginning and end of the lines.
Long texts set like this are difficult to read.
Centrally aligned texts are used for formal invitations,
introductory mottoes, quotations, etc.

This text is left ragged. The lines are aligned down the
right margin and the beginnings of the
lines are ragged.
This alignment is also unsuitable for longer texts,
as it is difficult to read.
Left ragged alignment is often used for captions.

This text is aligned down the left margin and is right ragged. Left aligned texts must be set with a font size that is suitable for the line width, because otherwise there can easily be large holes at the end of the lines, giving the text an unsettled appearance.

This text is also left aligned, but as a modified right ragged text. Like justified text it uses the available space well, but it avoids the disadvantage of large gaps between words. The disadvantage of modified right ragged alignment is that it is time-consuming to produce, but the result is very good to read.

Alignment and legibility

The alignment affects the overall impression created by a text. The appropriate alignment should be chosen for a given application: a newspaper will normally be fully justified – the text is spread over the full width of the column. A book may be aligned or right ragged – different lines have slightly different lengths to avoid overuse of hyphens. A formal invitation card, though, would generally have a central alignment. Left-ragged text is usually very difficult to read for any one used to reading from right to left.

1.06

Leading

The length of lines has to be matched to the spacing between the lines: The longer the lines then the greater the space needed between them.

»Typography primarily has a practical goal,
and only secondarily an aesthetic one...
This means that every typographic layout is wrong which,
for whatever reason,
places itself between the author and the reader.«
Stanley Morison

Frutiger Bold

Typography
Typography

Typography Typography

Base line

Ascender height

Cap height   X-height

Descender height

1
1.5   120%

Medium spacing

Headline without **leading**

Headline without **leading**

Headline leading without

Leading – space between lines

In order to make a text easy to read and to create the right overall impression, it is important to have the right space between lines. This is known as leading.

If the line spacing is insufficient, the text is difficult to distinguish for the reader. However, text without any leading can be used to achieve striking effects, and is quite common in advertising as a way of attracting attention: the text becomes a sculpture.

If too much leading is introduced between lines then this breaks up the text and all continuity is lost. The reader's attention is diverted to the gap between lines, and the text becomes an irritating combination of positive and negative elements. The line spacing should be chosen so that the lines are perceived but not the spaces between them. The line spacing, measured between the base line and the top of the lower case letters on the line below should measure between 100–150% of the height of lower case letters (x-height). The »automatic line spacing« of common computer programs has a default setting of 120%.

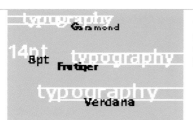

When choosing a typeface for the screen it is advisable to pay attention to the x-height: the more generous this is then the easier it will be to read the final product.

Frutiger Bold

Typography

Garamond

Typography

Even if they have the same cap height, different typefaces can have different medium heights. This can affect the overall impression created by a typeface considerably. The typeface which is on average higher (Frutiger) seems larger than the shorter one (Garamond). Although the font size and line spacing are the same (e.g. font size 10 pt, leading 12 pt) the optical effect is very different.

For long lines the line spacing should be greater than for short lines. This makes it easier for the eye to jump to the start of the next line.

This short sentence is written without leading.

This short sentence has been set to overlap.

Texts that overlap or have no leading can be very difficult to read.

This short sentence is written with normal eading.

If viewed from a distance, a body of text set with a »normal« line spacing is seen as a grey area without white horizontal bars. The more even the colour, then the better impact of forms of emphasis such as italics, bold, etc.

This short sentence is

written with extra

If the spacing between lines is too great the text loses all rhythm and seems unsettled. Additional leading is not appropriate for a body of text, but can be used as an interesting effect for short introductory texts.

leading.

1.07

Columns

The correct line length and appropriate text quantity for the screen have a positive effect on the ease with which the text will be read and understood.

»Printing is for a manuscript as the theatre is for women: it highlights the beauty but also shows up the faults – it can kill and bring to life.«

Honoré de Balzac

20 words per line or more

When the format has been selected and a typeface has been chosen for closer consideration, the next step is to create the grid. First of all, the column width is defined to enable the text to be read easily. The type size is closely linked with the column width. For good legibility of texts, the column should contain seven to ten words per line. The language of the texts is also an important consideration: German needs more space than Italian or English. If the column is too wide or too narrow, the reader tires quickly. If a column contains more than ten words per line, the text is more difficult to read because the eye loses itself in the length of the column. For very short texts, however, there can be fewer words per line without the text appearing fragmented.
But narrow columns should not be too long, because this impairs the reader's concentration on the text. If the columns are too short, the eye is distracted and jumps to the next column.

7–10 words per line

mi

mii

When the format has been selected and a typeface has been chosen for closer consideration, the next step is to create the grid. First of all, the column width is defined to enable the text to be read easily. The type size is closely linked with the column width. For good legibility of texts, the column should contain seven to ten words per line. The language of the texts is also an important consideration: German needs more space than Italian or English. If the column is too wide or too narrow, the reader tires quickly. If a column contains more than ten words per line, the text is more difficult to read because the eye loses itself in the length of the column. For very

short texts, however, there can be fewer words per line without the text appearing fragmented. But narrow columns should not be too long, because this impairs the reader's concentration on the text. If the columns are too short, the eye is distracted and jumps to the next column. The designer must use his discretion to decide how long the column should be; this depends on elements which are closely related in their effects: the column width, the typeface, the type size and the correct line spacing. The leading is a very important criterion which has a decisive effect on the legibility of texts.

If the leading is too narrow, the text tends to »stick together«, but if it is too wide this tends to produce »white bars« between the lines. The space between the letters should always be slightly less than the space between the lines. The leading itself is closely linked with the gap between columns. According to Manfred Simoneit, the letters »mi« – in the same typeface and type size as the type in the column – should fit between the columns. If the columns are separated by a line, at least »mii« should fit between them. If the leading for a text is large, this »mi« rule no longer applies and the gap between columns must be greater.

Column width, column spacing and column length

A text can be read comfortably if there are seven to ten words on a line. If a column is too wide or too narrow then the reader will soon become tired very quickly. With more than ten words on a line the text becomes harder to read because the eye loses its way: For short texts, however, fewer words can be placed on each line without any significant negative effects.

However, narrow columns should not be used for longer texts as this taxes the concentration of the reader. If columns are too short, reading is difficult because the eye has to jump from the bottom of one column to the top of the next one. It is a matter of judgement for the designer to decide how long a column should be, taking into account the associated elements: the width of the column, the typeface, the font size, and the appropriate line spacing.

The text in the first example on the right is very difficult to read because the lines are too long. The three short blocks in the example on the far right are easier to read.

4—5

words per line

When the format has been selected and a typeface has been chosen for closer consideration, the next step is to create the grid. First of all, the column width is defined to enable the text to be read easily. The type size is closely linked with the column width. For good legibility of texts, the column should contain seven to ten words per line. The language of the texts is also an important consideration: German needs more space than Italian or English. If the column is too wide or too narrow, the reader tires quickly.

with large leading

When the format has been

selected and a typeface has

been chosen for closer

consideration, the next step

is to create the grid. First

of all, the column width is

defined to enable the text

to be read easily. The type

size is closely linked with

the column width.

with small leading

When the format has been selected and a typeface has been chosen for closer consideration, the next step is to create the grid. First of all, the column width is defined to enable the text to be read easily. The type size is closely linked with the column width. For good legibility of texts, the column should contain seven to ten words per line.

The grid elements are interdependent:
Page format
Selection of typeface
Choice of font
Line spacing
Margins | Type area

Column widths of forty to fifty characters a line are ideal for normal text.

Long lines with more than fifty characters need larger line spacing but for shorter lines this is not necessary.

Wide columns produce a more harmonic impression than narrow columns because the letters are spread over the page better. But wide columns are harder to read, because the eye finds it difficult to return to the start of the next line. If the lines are too short, the overall impression is unsettled and the text is difficult to read because of frequent line changes.

The smaller the font size then the larger the line spacing should be. Conversely, the larger the font size, the closer the lines can come together.

1.08

With the international user in mind, the terms used should be easy to understand.

»Other countries,
other customs.«
German saying

The style differs from country to country

Numbers style	2 000.00	2,000.00	2.000,00	2´000,00	2 000,00	2,000 00
	International numbers style	Anglo-American numbers style | UK, USA, Canada, China	Continental numbers style | Germany, Italy	Switzerland	Finland, France	Japan

Telephone numbers

01-12 34 56 78   0 30-2 34-56 78   0033-1-123.456.78   0033.123.456-7891

The styles for telephone numbers vary widely. In the Continental style, the number is presented in blocks of two. Dialling codes are separated from the local number.

Internationally, numbers are often divided into blocks of three from left to right.
In general, numbers with more than four digits will be separated into groups of three digits.

Dates

YY-MM-DD   03-12-09   MM-DD-YY   12-09-03   DD.MM.YY   09.12.03

Dates are either presented in DD.MM.YY or MM/DD/YY formats. Years are now increasingly shown with four digits to avoid confusion.

The international date format starts with the largest unit, the year, followed by the month and then the day; for single-digit numbers an 0 is prefixed. A point or slash is used as a separator.

Quotation marks

»a«   „a"   «a»   "a"

French, Danish opening and closing quotation marks.

German opening and closing quotation marks.

Spanish, Italian, French, Norwegian, Portuguese opening and closing quotation marks.

Anglo-American opening and closing quotation marks.

Numerical expressions

3rd 3.   3te   3^e

Anglo-American   German   French

International terms

Typographic style rules apply for numbers, concepts and special characters. These rules differ from country to country: if they are familiar it becomes possible to identify the significance of a row of numbers from their layout, e.g. a bank account number.

If a non-standard style is used it can make it difficult to understand what is meant, or lead to misunderstandings.

100 700 00 BLZ
1 234 567 KTO

The subdivision into blocks of three is typical for bank sorting codes and account numbers. The sorting code is divided from left to right, but the account number is divided from right to left.

Long – and short – dashes

Hy-
phen

The hyphen is short and is placed directly behind the first part of a word that is hyphenated.
The dash is the same length as a minus sign and slightly longer than a hyphen. It is used with a gap between the words, particularly subordinate clauses in sentences.

1 + 1 = 2

In a mathematical formula, gaps should be inserted between the numbers and symbols.

A more harmonious effect is achieved with numbers if the digits are set closer together than letters.

All terms should be easily understood by Internet users all over the world. But not only do the terms differ, care must also be taken with the use of colours, because their connotations can differ widely from culture to culture.

For example, pink: In Europe it stands for softness and being childish, but in Korea it stands for trust.

Definitions

Antique face	Typeface with serifs
Ascender	The part of lower case letters which projects above the x-height
Bitmap type	Typeface made up of pixels
Body type	Main typeface used for body text in books and newspapers; all typefaces except headings and marginal notes
Body width	Overall width of a letter
Cap line	Height of capital letters, »H«
Centred type	Text aligned around a central axis
Counter	Space within letters, e.g. in an »O«
Didot point	Measurement unit for type size (0.375 mm/abbreviation: dd)
DTP point	Measurement unit for type size (0.352 mm/abbreviation: pt)
Egyptienne	A serif typeface without hairlines, but with bold down strokes
Fraktur	Gothic type
Fully justified text	Text with lines that cover the full column width
Grotesque face	Sans serif typeface, typeface without serifs
Gutter	(US) Distance between columns
Interlinear spacing	Space between one line and the next
Kerning	Reduced spacing between letters
Left justified	Text with a straight left edge, follows the normal reading flow
Legibility	Criteria: interlinear spacing, type size, tracking, line length
Line length	Column width
Majuscule	Upper case letter, capital letter
Marginal notes	Notes in the margin
Minuscule	Lower case letter, small letter
Modified ragged	Ragged typesetting with hyphenation
Pictogram	Visual symbol that can be understood in any language
Ragged text	Typesetting with varying line lengths
Right justified	Text with a straight right edge and a ragged left edge, goes against the flow of reading in western cultures
Sans serif	Typeface without serifs
Small caps	Letters which have the height of an »x« and the shape of a capital
Style	Bold, semi-bold, normal, light, italic
Tracking	Spacing between the letters
Upper case	Capital letters
Wide spacing	Increased spacing between letters
Word spacing	Space between the individual words (quad)

a
b
c
def
g
ikl
m
pr
st
uw

2

Do classic typographic rules apply on screen?
What are the appropriate colours, type sizes,
trackings, text quantities, line lengths and line
spacing for the screen?

Colours

On the screen, colours are generated by means of light. The additive colour system, which supports the screen is composed of the primary colours red, green and blue (**RGB**).

»...I can´t make up my mind, everything is so beautiful and colourful here! I gawk at the tv!«
Nina Hagen

Additive colour system

Primary colours
R | Red
G | Green
B | Blue

Secondary colours
C | Cyan
M | Magenta
Y | Yellow

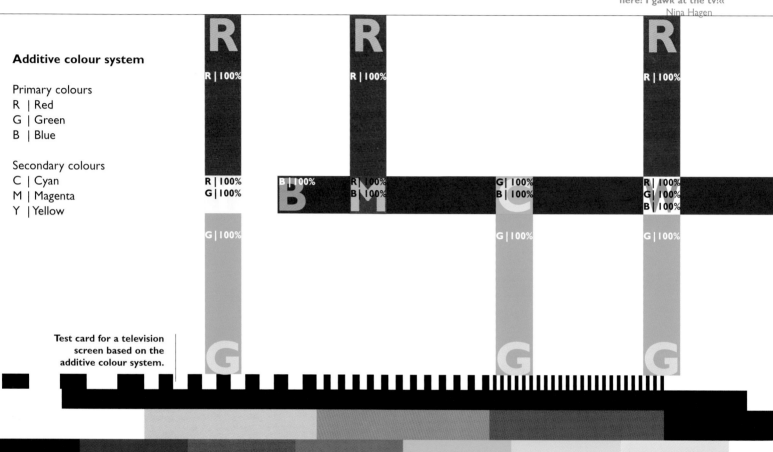

Test card for a television screen based on the additive colour system.

Additive colour system

The principle colours (also primary colours) of the additive colour system are red, green and blue. These three colours, when mixed together with equal intensity, appear white.

The secondary colours (resulting mix of two primary colours of equal intensity) of the additive colour system are cyan, magenta and yellow.

The additive colour system is composed of light. The absence of all colours results in black. On the screen, colours are created from the principle colours of the additive colour system (RGB) by means of light impulses.

The represention of colours on the screen is subject to tolerance: the appearance can differ greatly according to product and make. Red can vary between red and orange, green shifts to lime and blue to violet. These variations in tone of the primary colours then affect all other mixtures. Thus, when working with digital media, the designer can only provide a »recommendation« of sorts and cannot assume that the viewer will see the same colours.

Light-generated representation and contrast of colour often comes across with greater intensity than that effected through pigment. The designer must therefore take particular care to avoid excessive brightness on the screen, this applies especially to typefaces and texts which are to be read.

C | 100%

C | 100%

C | 100%

C | 100%

C | 100%
K
M | 100%
R
C | 100%
B
M | 100%
M
C | 100%
G

C | 100%
M | 100%
Y | 100%

M | 100%
Y | 100%

C | 100%
M | 100%

M | 100%

Subtractive colour system

Primary colours
C | Cyan
M | Magenta
Y | Yellow
(K | Black)

Secondary colours
R | Red
G | Green
B | Blue

Test card for print-outs based on the subtractive colour system.

Um. rein Thiessen 12.03. 16:44 Uhr Seite 1 (Schwarz Bogen)

Subtractive colour system

The principle colours (also primary colours) of the subtractive colour system are cyan, magenta and yellow. These three colours, when mixed together with equal intensity, appear black.

The secondary colours (resulting mix of two primary colours of equal intensity) of the subtractive colour system are red, green and blue.

The subtractive colour system makes use of »physical« colours composed of pigment, the additive colour system, on the other hand, comprises light-based (colour) elements. In the subtractive colour system, colours are perceived due to reflected light (absorption and reflection). When, for example, a book is printed, the subtractive colour system forms the basis. The three primary colours, when mixed together, form a kind of dark brown rather than a true pitch black and therefore black (K) is included separately, hence the CMYK-print format.

»The mixture arising from bad colours,
even if chosen exactly on the basis of the colour spectrum,
is not a white colour, but more like mud.«
Dziga Vertov

2.02

The effects of colours

Colours can have different significance in different countries and societies. In worldwide communications, for example with the Internet, this culture-specific interpretation of colour represents a real challenge for designers.

»Red is blood, red is the colour of alarm, [...] of wounds, the poppy, anger and shame, red is many things, the plush in the theatre, [...] the pope, [...] the devil is red, allegedly, and red is born of green yes, of all colours, it has to be red – for Gantenbein.«
Max Frisch

The significance of colours in different cultures

Black

	USA		Asia		South America		...but also:	
USA	Mourning	Asia	Power	China	South America	Mourning	...but also:	Clever
Europe	Pessimism		Money	China		Death		Sublime
	Jealousy	France		Mourning		Secret		Valuable
	Hunger	Portugal						

White

USA	Innocence	Asia	Mourning	China, Japan	South America	Peace	...but also:	Elegance
Europe	Purity		Death	China, Japan		Cleanliness		Sobriety
	Lack of success	Italy				Purity		Sterility
	Quality	Sweden						

Grey

USA	Sterility	Asia	Inexpressive	Japan	South America	Objectivity	...but also:	Boredom
Europe	Sobriety		Sadness	Korea				
			Negative feelings	Korea				

Red

USA	Love	Asia	Happiness	China	South America	Anger		
Europe	Anger		Fame	China		Warmth		
	Passion		Wealth	China		Violence		
	Pleasure	France	Aggression	Japan				
			Femininity	Japan				

Violet

USA	Sensuality	Asia	Prostitution				...but also:	Dubious
Europe	Death							Lonely
	Esoteric							
	Mysticism							

The effects of colour

In different cultures, different colours can come to have very different meanings. The development of associations will often depend on the availability of the substances that can be used to produce a colour, as well as on the frequency of the colour in the natural surroundings. For example, green is not often found in nature in Arabic countries and it is regarded as symbolising strength.

The differing and sometimes contradictory effects of colours in different cultures means that designers of websites have to be extremely careful when choosing the colours they use. The challenge is to find a colour that produces more or less uniform associations internationally – without producing any unpleasant surprises.

The garish colours of the website for the Berlin Love Parade not only attract a younger public than the grey used in the design of the Audi site, but they also transmit different values: the Love Parade aims to be loud and poppy, whereas Audi want to appear serious and controlled.

With the choice of the main colours (e.g. the background colour) and the colours that are combined with it (e.g. the colour of the typeface) the designer of a website can influence the response of the user.

Blue

USA	Faithfulness	**Asia**	Care	**South America**	Tranquillity
Europe	Masculinity		Caution		Coldness
	Coldness		Faithfulness		Indifference
	Fear | Italy, France				

Arabian	Virtue
countries	Trust
	Truth

Yellow

USA	Envy	**Asia**	Wisdom | China	**South America**	Happiness
Europe	Jealousy		Patience | China		Sun
	Caution		Dignity | Japan		Envy
	Energy		Nobility | Japan		Illness

Arabian	Happiness
countries	Wealth

Green

USA	Nature-loving	**Asia**	Hope	**South America**	Immaturity
Europe	Harmony		Tranquillity		Hope
	Hope		Energy | Japan		Freedom
	Pettiness | Germany		Fear | Malaysia		Illness
	Shortage of money | Italy				

Arabian	Fertility
countries	Strength

Pink

USA	Tenderness	**Asia**	Trust	**South America**	Sweetness
Europe	Care				
	Femininity				
	Kitsch				

Arabian	Feminine
countries	Effeminate

Melancholic	**Blue**	Sensible	Exaggerated	**Yellow**	Extrovert	Reserved	**Turquoise**	Refreshing
		Profound	Vain		Joyful	Sterile		

The way a colour is perceived also depends on the mood of the viewer, and their personal experience.

Colours are rarely used in isolation. But when they are used in combination with other colours each one influences the other. If you cover two of the squares to the left and look at the remaining one in combination with the background you will be able to appreciate this effect: the green of the background seems much fresher with the white square than with the black one.

The designer can already transmit a basic mood by the choice of colours.
Typical uses of colours in North America and western Europe include:

Activity | Red, Orange, Yellow
Honesty | White, Blue, Green
Functionality | White, Grey, Black
Ideal | White, Blue, Gold
Cleverness | White, Blue, Silver
Performance | Blue, Gold, Red
Innovation | Violet, Orange, Silver
Objectivity | White, Grey, Blue
Speed | Silver, Red, Yellow
Security | Green, White, Blue
Likeable | Blue, Red, Green
Trust | Blue, Green, White
Reliability | Blue, Green, Brown

2.02

Colour contrasts

040.**041**

Colours act as points of reference for one another: they can form harmonious, mutually-complementary relationships or create contrasts.
The colour-temperature contrast allows the creation of harmonious relationships.

»I find myself permanently mindful of the laws of colour.
If only we had been taught these properly in our student years«
Vincent van Gogh

1.1 Warm and warm contrast   1.2 Cold and cold contrast

The website of the Vitra Design Museum is composed of warm, friendly colours communicating positivity and openness.

The Vitra Des
museums in the world. One of
collections of modern furnitu
international travelling-exhi
and workshops. Our Museum Sho
publications, a unique Miniat

The website of West Coast Retreats is composed of fresh colours implying purity and refreshment. If the page appeared in the colours of the Vitra site, the viewer would come away more with the impression of a beach holiday in the sun rather than one of revitalising invigoration.

Colour contrasts

Colours seldom appear in isolation. The effect a colour gives off is always determined by the colours with which it is contrasted: one colour can thus act in a wide variety of ways upon the viewer according to how it is combined.
Choice of colours and their arrangement in relation to each other can alone be enough to relay a message and capture the attention of a specific target group. When someone is looking for a bank with a view to paying in money, he or she expects frankness, reliability and seriousness. Any bank choosing to present itself in leafy green and orange simply won't come across with the same authority as a bank using, say, greys, blues or light-coloured tones. Qualities such as tone (colour frequency), brightness (the addition of white, i.e. light or conversely the addition of black, i.e. reduction of light), saturation (intensity/purity) and the quantity in which the colour appears are other factors influencing the way a colour works: an intense red and a pink will affect the viewer quite differently.

The effect of an intense red can be changed by altering its brightness: here, white (i.e. light) is added.

The square on the left has a higher saturation (colour-purity level), hence the increased strength when compared to the square on the right.

Qualities of a colour:
tone
brightness
saturation

Colour interplay:
complementary contrast
harmony
dischord
colour temperature

1.3 Warm and cold contrast

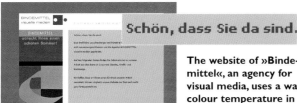

The website of »Binde-
mittel«, an agency for
visual media, uses a warm
colour temperature in
its presentation. The
presence of quantitively
smaller amounts of
cold colour sets off a
highly-charged contrast
without allowing the
overall impression of
warmth to be lost.

The website of Mahaina
Wellness Resorts uses
basic colours in its fresh-
looking presentation
while contrasting them
with warm elements.

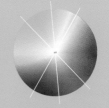

Temperature contrast (1.1–1.3)
Colours can be divided into warm and cold types
depending on how high their temperature is.
Warm colours, those provoking a sense of
warmth and openness, comprise the range of
tone variations from red through to yellow on
the colour wheel. Warm colours, when combined
with each other, act to create proximity, a sense
of well-being and seem charged with energy (1.1).
Cold colours, those conveying a feeling of cool
seriousness, are to be found between the range
of tone variations from green through to blue on
the colour wheel. Cold colours, when combined
with each other, act to create distance and
impersonality but at the same time an impression
of seriousness and functionality (1.2).
The combination of warm and cold colours can
produce powerful contrasts. The temperature
represented in the greater quantity determines
the overall impression (1.3).

2.02

Colour contrasts

Through use of chromatic-achromatic (colour-monochrome) contrasts, unobtrusive, harmonious arrangements can be achieved providing that a pure colour is not contrasted with a black-white monochrome scheme.
Complementary colour contrasts are highly evocative and can occasionally appear aggressive. They should therefore be used sparingly and with careful consideration.

»A colour doesn't exist unless defined by a language.«
Jean Baudrillard

2.1 Chromatic-achromatic contrast

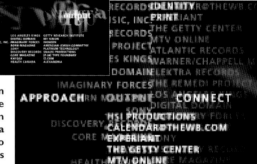

The dark red used on the Fuse website is just right for the white typeface and, despite the dark hue of the background, the impression is one of freshness.

The achromatic design of the website www.typographic.com uses colour solely as a means of contrast to divert attention towards the site's interactive features.

Colour contrasts

Chromatic-achromatic contrasts (2.1)
Achromatic monochrome (white, black and the range of tones between) combines very well with colour. The resulting effect is one of colour but not of loudness, leaving an impression of unobtrusive stability. Contrasts of this type are a good basis on which to create balanced layouts provided that pure colours are not combined with black. Yellow and black or red and black are two such combinations, appearing very intense and resulting in a signal character. It is clear why they are often used in road signs or found in nature as with the wasp's warning sign of danger with its stripes.

If a black or white space surrounds a coloured one, the coloured area of the screen will appear very intense. This is due to the intensity of the colour working alone.

Intensive contrasts, e.g.
complementary colour
contrasts, are very well
suited to attracting
attention, say on a
home page. It is this same
intensity, though, that
makes them unsuitable
as main themes.

3.1 Complementary colour contrast

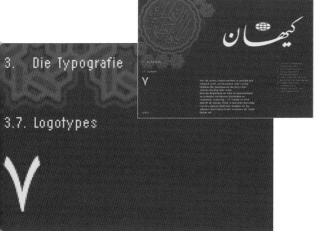

In this **CD-ROM** on
Persian script, gold-
coloured highlighting
of themes forms a
complementary
relationship with the
blue background. **Here,
the stark contrast is
not disagreeable to
the eye because of the
counteractive calming
effect of the blue.**

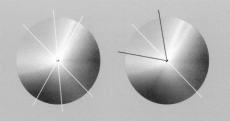

Used on a home page,
a sharp contrast of
complementary colours
can arouse interest and
create an impression of
unconventionality as
here on the website of
»Unpublished – The Best
Rejected Advertising«.

Complementary colour contrasts (3.1)
These colour tones are to be found opposite
each other on the colour wheel and result in
stark contrasts and impressions of dissonance –
these combinations of colours will appear very
intense, garish and loud. A less-intense variation on
the complementary colour contrast is the »semi-
complementary colour contrast« in which the
colour next to the complementary colour is used.

2.02

Colour contrasts

044.045

Monochrome colour contrasts create an introverted effect. Alone, they may come across as lacking in energy and should therefore be combined with a third, contrasting colour.
Colours vary in character according to their environment. This phenomenon is called simultaneous contrast.

»...colour is that aspect of nature's uniformity
that is relevant to the eye.«
Johann Wolfgang von Goethe

4.1 Contrast of tone

4.2 Contrast of quality

5.1 Consecutively-positioned tones

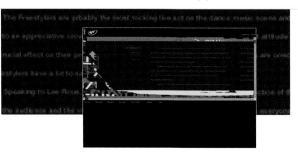

Using contrast of quality (i.e. by varying light strength) the secondary information recedes and the buttons are emphasised.

More extensive texts can be hard on the eye if rendered in a monochromatic, tone-based contrast. The difference between the pure colour and its lighter counterweight has to be fairly significant in order to ensure legibility.

The close affinity of khaki green and beige create an unobtrusive foundation for use as a background. The white lettering stands out well against this background due to the clear contrast.

Colour contrasts

Monochromatic colour contrasts allow the creation of smooth-looking compositions. Layout elements such as logos can easily be integrated in a way that is discrete. Important information is best rendered in a colour contrasting clearly with the background.

Monochrome colour contrast
Schemes using only monochrome colours will result in mutually weak contrasts. One advantage is that their similarity makes them easy to combine.

Contrast of tone (4.1) and
Contrast of quality (4.2)
Contrast of tone (light-dark contrast), consisting of a pure colour and its lighter counterweight, as well as contrast of quality, the term used to describe the varying luminescence of colours, produce well-balanced effects. There is, however, the danger of them lacking in vibrance.

Consecutively-postioned tones (5.1)
These are colour tones found near each other on the colour wheel. Such combinations, as with contrasts of tone and quality, form a good basis on which to create a balanced layout. When contrasted with a further colour, the result can be one of rich vibrancy founded on a harmonious structure.

The careful arrangement of colours will create order and give the impression of balance; too many colours will confuse.

6.1.1 Simultaneous contrast   **6.**1.2   **6.**1.3   **6.**1.4

The differing effects of red against a variety of backgrounds.

6.2 Contrast of quantity

Against the blue background, the orange stripe seems more powerful than the smaller orange spot,

which, while apparently lighter, seems less colour intensive. Against the orange background, the

narrow blue stripe produces a less colourful effect and seems darker than the broader stripe.

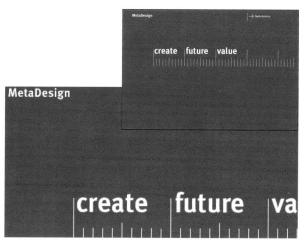

Red and red are not the same: Red is a colour provoking strong emotions. It can just as easily stand for love as it can for combat. The character of red changes, depending on the colour with which it is combined. Used in combination with white, it seems dynamic and fresh.

Red combined with black comes across as forceful and overbearing.

Simultaneous contrast (6.1)
Colours vary in character according to their environment. This phenomenon is called simultaneous contrast.
The following standard shifts in effect can be observed: Achromatic boarders increase the luminescence of a colour (**6.**1.1). Seen against a dark background, colour appears lighter than when set against a pale background. A pale background will force a colour to the foreground, while a darker background will cause it to recede again (**6.**1.2). A cold colour, if enclosed by a warm-coloured boarder will appear cooler than it actually is, whereas the same colour, instead set within a cold boarder, will appear warmer (**6.**1.3). A colour taken from a position consecutive on the colour wheel to that of the foreground colour will, if used as a background, decrease the prominence of the foreground colour. The more complementary the background colour, in terms of its position on the colour wheel, the purer and more luminous the foreground colour will seem (**6.**1.4).

Contrast of quantity (6.2)
Contrast of quantity refers to the variations in appearance of a colour brought about by factors of quantitative distribution.

Johann Wolfgang von Goethe attempted to assign a value to each colour based on »optical« units of weight. He came up with the following list:

yellow: 9 units
orange: 8
red: 6
green: 6
blue: 4
violet: 3

According to this scheme, the colour yellow is three times »heavier« than the colour violet. In order that the violet might act as a balancing counterweight to the yellow, it would, says Goethe, have to be represented by a total area three times greater than that represented by the yellow. Used with red or green, it would need to be twice as big.

2.02

Text and colour contrast

046.**047**

When combining text with a background, it is possible to avoid both flicker-effects and excessive brightness provided great care is taken in atuning the combinations. Colour quality, brightness, saturation and contrast each play an important role.

»Cast away this script,
it makes you cold and unfeeling,
it will surely turn your heart to stone.«
Ludwig Tieck

type for the screen	type for the screen	type for the screen	type for the screen
and for other digital media	and for other digital media	and for other digital media	and for other digital media

1.1 **Achromatic-contrast**
White | Black

1.2 White | Black 80%

1.3 Black 80% | White

1.4 Black 60% | White

type for the screen	type for the screen	type for the screen	type for the screen
and for other digital media	and for other digital media	and for other digital media	and for other digital media

2.1 **Achromatic-chromatic contrast**
Black | Cyan

2.2 Black | Magenta

2.3 Black | Yellow

2.4 White | Yellow

type for the screen	type for the screen	type for the screen	type for the screen
and for other digital media	and for other digital media	and for other digital media	and for other digital media

3.1 **Achromatic-chromatic contrast**
Black | R 40%, G 55%, B 65%

3.2 Black | R 80%, G 45%, B 45%

3.3 Black | R 100%, G 70%, B 2%

3.4 Red | R 100%, G 70%, B 2%

Text and Colour Contrast

On the screen, colour contrasts come across with greater intensity than they would in print format because the colours consist of light rather than material.

The eye has grown used to seeing in traditional print format, black type on a white background, a combination of limited suitability for use on the screen (1.1). There is more than one reason for this: white is represented on the screen by means of the additive colour system, that is to say by each colour emitting light at full intensity, further, when black is used as text against this very bright background, the result is a stark contrast similar to the colour-complementary contrast. Both factors are hard on the eye.

One way of reducing contrast is to render the text in dark grey on the white background (1.2). White lettering on a grey screen similarly lowers the contrast (1.3, 1.4) – because of the much-reduced brightness of the background, the eye is under less strain. Otherwise, the white lettering can be set against a black (i.e. light-free) background (1.6). The contrast can then be optimised by altering the text colour to between a light or medium grey (1.5, 1.7, 1.8).

For some viewers, the combination of white or grey text on a black or dark-grey background feels drab or overbearing. If the black background is combined with a primary or a secondary colour (2.1–2.3, 2.5–2.7), the resulting effects, while undoubtedly full of optical vitality, nevertheless have an unconvincing feel to them. There is also the danger of excessive brightness and flicker-effect due to the great intensity of the pure colour. A white background, combined with a pure colour appears shrill (2.4) and can, because of the intensive emission of light and the brightness of the backgound, even render a text illegible (2.8, 3.8).

On a black background, it is preferable to use a tertiary colour of low saturation (3.1–3.3, 3.5: in comparison with high saturation) or to replace the black background with a grey one (3.6, 3.7). Care must still be taken to ensure that the grey is not of a similar brightness to the colour, otherwise there will be a lack of contrast and the text, particularly smaller type, will be hard to read (3.7).

Black backgrounds promote readability on the screen. Black on the screen means that there is no light being emitted. This reduces the chances of flicker-effect.

With white backgrounds, legibility can be a problem: flicker-effects tend to occur very easily. This is due to the representation of colour on the screen being based on light emission. White is produced when red, green and blue are mixed at full intensity.

Grey backgrounds with white lettering result in very good readability. Indeed, this works just as well if the lettering is in a less-intensive tertiary colour. Nevertheless, if grey is used, it should not be of a similar brightness to that of the grey background.

type for the screen	type for the screen	type for the screen	type for the screen
and for other digital media	and for other digital media	and for other digital media	and for other digital media
1.5 Black 50% | White	1.6 Black | White	1.7 Black | Black 50%	1.8 Black | Black 10%

type for the screen	type for the screen	type for the screen	type for the screen
and for other digital media	and for other digital media	and for other digital media	and for other digital media
2.5 Black | Red	2.6 Black | Green	2.7 Black | Blue	2.8 White | Blue

type for the screen	type for the screen	type for the screen	type for the screen
and for other digital media	and for other digital media	and for other digital media	and for other digital media
3.5 Black | Green	3.6 Black 80% | Green	3.7 Black 30% | Green	3.8 White | Green

Paper

A black letter on the page comes across more strongly than a white letter on a black printed background.
The reasons for this lie in the absorbancy of the paper.
With smaller type, there is the danger of detailed serifs or linear intensity of the letter being lost against the back-ground.

On the screen, the precise opposite is true. Unlike material, the white background is not perceptible because of its reflected light but rather the whiteness of the surface is caused by the additive colour mixture emitting the maximum possible light. This means that a black letter (composed of »dead light«) appears faint against the background, while a white letter on a black screen appears to have more energy because of the intensity of the light. Black letters in small-sized type against a white background can lack intensity,

even if used only for text boxes. The black-white contrast is far more intense on the screen than on paper. Far more suitable as a reading format is a dark blue background with light-coloured text – assuming, that is, that the designer is not trying to simulate paper, but is approaching the screen as a medium in its own right, complete with its own laws and attributes.

Screen

The readability of a text is not only affected by the defining factors of typeface and type size, but also of colour contrast between the text and the background.

»Truly, man's ability to comprehend
is without limit.«
Werner Heisenberg

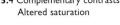

4.1 Chromatic-achromatic contrast
Red | Black

4.2   Red | Black 80%

4.3   Red | Black 10%

4.4   Red 70% | Black

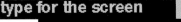

5.1 Complementary contrasts

5.2 Complementary contrasts

5.3 Complementary contrasts

5.4 Complementary contrasts
Altered saturation

6.1 Light-dark contrasts
Dark background

6.2 Light-dark contrasts
Reverse of 6.1

6.3 Light-dark contrasts
Light background

6.4 Light-dark contrasts
Dark background

Text and Colour Contrast

Similar guidelines apply to a pure-coloured background when used with black lettering: the luminescense of the pure colour is far too bright as a background for the black type (**4.1**). Dark-grey lettering on a background of pure colour is far more pleasant to read (**4.2**). The contrast between a pure colour and white comes across as even more pronounced. If, instead of pure white lettering, a slightly off-white tone is used, the resulting lower contrast enhances readability (**4.3**). The same is true for black lettering set on a reduced pure colour (**4.4**). Tertiary colours with high levels of intrinsic brightness are better suited for use as backgrounds, and can even be combined with black (**4.5**). The effect can be optimised if the black is replaced by a dark grey (**4.6**).

To ensure good readability, the designer must take care to ensure that the contrasts are neither too strong (**1.1**, **2.2–2.4**, **2.8**, **3.8**) nor too weak (**4.7**, **4.8**).

Complementary contrasts come across on the screen with greater intensity than on printed paper because the colours are composed of mixtures of light. The resulting visual sensation is – due to the strength of the light emitted and the purity of the colours – exceptionally well suited to drawing attention but not easily adapted to the presentation of text (**5.1–5.3**). The flicker-effect can make especially small and narrow segments of text as well as smaller lettering difficult or impossible to read due to excessive brightness at the edges. Complementary colours, being of high intrinsic brightness, can cause fine lines set against them to vanish almost entirely. If a visually-striking page is required, then the tonality or saturation of the complementary colour can be altered (**5.4**, **5.5**) or a semi-complementary contrast, i.e. a colour not directly opposite, used (**5.6–5.8**) so as to maintain an acceptable level of readability. The text becomes easier to read without the overall effect being lost.

type for the screen
and for other digital media

type for the screen
and for other digital media

type for the screen
and for other digital media

type for the screen
and for other digital media

4.5 R 55%, G 80%, B 10% | Black

4.6 R 55%, G 80%, B 10% | Black 80%

4.7 R 55%, G 80%, B 10% | Black 30%

4.8 R 55%, G 80%, B 10% | Black 10%

type for the screen
and for other digital media

type for the screen
and for other digital media

type for the screen
and for other digital media

type for the screen
and for other digital media

5.5 Complementary contrasts
Altered saturation

5.6 Semi-complementary contrast

5.7 Semi-complementary contrast

5.8 Semi-complementary contrast

type for the screen
and for other digital media

type for the screen
and for other digital media

type for the screen
and for other digital media

type for the screen
and for other digital media

6.5 Light-dark contrasts
Medium-dark background

6.6 Light-dark contrasts
Medium-dark background

6.7 Light-dark contrasts
Equal brightness

6.8 Light-dark contrasts
Light background

The light-dark contrast of using light-coloured lettering set against a darker-coloured background is very pleasant to the eye: the closer the background colour is to black, the less light it emits (**6.**1, **6.**4, **6.**5).
So as to ensure that, despite the subdued background, the page still grabs the viewer's attention, the designer can select a lively tone for use as text colour (**6.**1, **6.**4). For shorter texts or on pages where the viewer is likely to move on fairly quickly, the colour combination can be reversed (**6.**2), or the text colour set against a white screen (**6.**3, **6.**8) so as to keep things looking fresh.
A medium-dark background is well suited to use as a base-theme and combines nicely with very dark (**6.**5) or very light colours (**6.**6). Using colours of equal brightness will, however, render the text illegible (**6.**7, **7.**1).

Intrinsic brightness

White — High

Yellow   Lime-green

Orange

Medium   Red   Green — Middle
grey

Violet

Blue

Black — Low

2.02

050.**051**

Text on structured backgrounds is in most cases very difficult to read. This is best used only as an »eye-catcher« rather than as a means of relaying information.

»I was flying with my mind, looking around me.
And I see there's no more room in my human thought
In the Internet.
Everything I get.
And the plastic dreams of what?«
Eiffel 65

7.1 Temperature contrast
Cold-cold contrast

7.2 Temperature contrast
Cold-cold contrast

7.3 Temperature contrast
Warm-warm contrast

7.4 Temperature contrast
Warm-warm contrast

9.1 Structured background

9.2 Structured background

9.3 Structured background

9.4 Structured background

9.9 Structured background

9.10 Structured background

9.11 Structured background

9.12 Structured background

Text and Colour Contrast

Very smooth-looking contrasts can be achieved using temperature contrasts (two colours of the same temperature taken from consecutive positions on the colour wheel). Here, the designer must pay special attention to levels of brightness, otherwise small type will not be readable (**7.1–7.4**).

Another kind of contrast that makes for a well-balanced theme is the tonal-based contrast (**8.1–8.4**). It's almost too harmonious to be read and tends to work better as a background theme that, when looked at more closely, allows information like, say, a background logo or a tag for a particular area of interest to be picked out.

A tone-in-tone contrast taken as background allows exciting structures to be played around with (**9.1, 9.4, 9.5–9.7, 9.9, 9.10**) and a feeling of depth created: a lighter tone stands out, while a darker tone appears further away (**9.2**).

For structured backgrounds, tone-in-tone contrasts are easy to handle and can have effective results when the designer overlays them with text. Difficulties arise in the case of non-homogeneous backgrounds, on which strong variations in brightness tend to show up (**9.1–9.3**). The information contained in the text quickly gets lost as the eye's attention is drawn to the background structure.

For the designer, being able to conceptualise digital media as an independent form of communication, and work with it accordingly, rather than thinking in terms of analogies with print, is an ongoing challenge. An integral part of this is the presentation of new visual formats, i.e. breaking away from the typical paper format of black text on white background.
Or do digital surfaces really need to look like fake real fires?

type for the screen
and for other digital media

8.1 Tone-in-tone contrast

type for the screen
and for other digital media

8.2 Tone-in-tone contrast

type for the screen
and for other digital media

8.3 Tone-in-tone contrast

type for the screen
and for other digital media

8.4 Tone-in-tone contrast

type for the screen
and for other digital media

9.5 Structured background

type for the screen
and for other digital media

9.6 Structured background

type for the screen
and for other digital media

9.7 Structured background

type for the screen
and for other digital media

9.8 Structured background

type for the screen
and for other digital media

9.13 Structured background

type for the screen
and for other digital media

9.14 Structured background

type for the screen
and for other digital media

9.15 Structured background

type for the screen
and for other digital media

9.16 Structured background

A grey tinted background is more interesting, and may provide secondary information. It makes the white font stand out clearly as the main carrier of information.

Another alternative: using frames to highlight text.

ideas are the currency of the future
➤ they solve problems
➤ they create opportunities

On a non-homogenous background, the font must be clearly differentiated: Here, the impact of the font in white is fresh and distinctive on dim hues of black and blue.

A R T I S T I C A
VISUAL DESIGN INNOVATION

2.03

Type sizes

052.**053**

Typeface sizes that can be read easily on paper are often too small for monitor screens, due to their poor resolution: The screen is a medium of its own with its own rules.

»When this multimedia develops into a sort of book, with which you can snuggle into bed, in order to amuse yourself or listen to a story.«
Nicholas Negroponte

typography for digital media

Helvetica, 9 pt

typography for digital media

Chicago, 9 pt

typography for digital media

Times, 12 pt

Times, 9 pt

typography for digital media

Helvetica, 12 pt

Chicago, 12 pt

The smaller the font size, the harder it is to distinguish the individual characters.

Helvetica, 9 pt

Helvetica, 7 pt

Chicago,

Helvetica, 12 pt

typography for digital media

Times, 12 pt

typography for digital media

Helvetica, 14 pt

typography for digital media

Helvetica, 16 p

Type sizes on screen

Various font sizes and styles should be tested before a font is used for screen text presentations. It is not always the case that the larger the font size then the easier it will be to read.

Font sizes that can be easily read on printed pages are not necessarily suitable for use on screens and displays. The presentation of text on a screen is in fact quite poor in comparison with printing due to the low screen resolution. Printing is possible at resolutions of 1200 or 2400 dpi (dots per inch), whereas on screen the resolution will not usually be more than 72 dpi or 96 dpi. The result is that small font sizes which can easily be read on paper, such as 6 point, are too fuzzy to read on a screen. As a general rule, font sizes smaller than 10 point should be avoided. It is preferable to use font sizes of 11 point to 14 point, with headlines and titles of 14 point to 20 point. Every font and font style needs to be considered individually. The larger the font size, the more pixels will be available to present each character. Presenting an image with picture elements offers a high degree of flexibility, but it has the disadvantage that the outlines have to be produced by combinations of vertical and horizontal lines.

The choice of type size depends among other things
on the nature of the background. If it is unsettled
or there is little contrast between background and
typeface then it is advisable to use a larger font.

typography for digital media
Helvetica, 36 pt

typography for digital media
Helvetica, 9 pt

typography for digital media
Chicago, 7 pt

typography for digital media
Times, 12 pt

typography for digital media
Chicago, 12 pt

typography for digital media
Helvetica, 12 pt

typography for digital media
Helvetica, 7 pt

typography for digit
Helvetica, 48 pt

typography for digital media
Helvetica, 7 pt

typography for digital media
Chicago, 7 pt

typography for digital media
Chicago, 7 pt

typography for digital media
Helvetica, 7 pt

typography for digital media
Helvetica, 16 pt

typography for digital media
Helvetica, 9 pt

typography for digital media
Helvetica, 8 pt

typography for digital media
Helvetica, 36 pt

typography for digital media
Chicago, 12 pt

typography for digital media
Chicago, 7 pt

typography for digital media
Helvetica, 7 pt

typography for digital media
Helvetica, 14 pt

As long as the screen continues to rely on today's poor standards of resolution, it is appropriate that design for the medium be based more around pictorial information than detailed reams of text.

»Pictures came and broke my heart. [...]
Video killed the radio star.«
The Buggles

Type corrupted to the point of unreadability:

Typography

Times 10 pt

Typography

Times 14 pt

Crisis management

Helvetica — set in Helvetica on screen

Helvetica — set in Univers on screen

Helvetica — set in Helvetica on paper

Helvetica — set in Univers on paper

Type on the screen as an oath of disclosure for the scope of the medium.
All the attention to detail and fineness that the trained eye of the designer has become used to transposing on to paper doesn't, for the most part, work on the screen. The kind of detail that sets good typographical design apart is – on grounds of the screen's low resolution – either not attempted at all or not done properly. And this applies to, of all media, the Internet – linked up to provide access from anywhere in the world and, as such, far more widely distributed and easier to update than a print product. For a medium that lays claim to »unlimited possibilities«, it does not allow much scope where typographical design is concerned. The designer is forced to put typographical considerations on the back burner and concentrate more on atmospheric effect, navigation, user-guidance and graphical representation. It has more to do with crisis management of the pixel than with passion for detail.

Crisis management is an approach that keeps the limitations of the medium in mind, aiming to find the best solution possible. Under no circumstances should the designer be attempting to directly transpose his or her print know-how on to the screen. An example would be the full range of smaller type sizes that are not available to the designer for use on screen if he or she intends to present the reader with an acceptably readable text. Moreover, many type styles either don't look good on screen, or cannot be differentiated between because of the coarseness of the representation. Choice of font is a factor just as crucial to readability as cleverly combined text colour and background. It is true that some of these deficiencies can now be improved somewhat through use of anti-aliasing effects on letters, yet, quite apart from criteria affecting readability, there is always one disquieting factor – that of the aesthetic quality falling just short: unattractive pixelisation or frayed edges on carefully laid-out letters is surely a slap in the face for any designer.

PTTPostBusiness.nl

When PTT Post was c
company by the Dutc
Dumbar was asked to
corporate visual ident

Clearly broken down,
concise blocks of text in
suitably-sized type, expres-
sive colour scheming and a
self-referential choice of

images can gloss over the
lack of scope offered by the
technology.

Typography

Helvetica 10 pt

Typography

Helvetica 14 pt

Typography

Univers 10 pt

Typography

Univers 14 pt

Particularly with small-
sized type, the finer
details of individual typefaces become difficult to
make out on screen.

From epoche to epoche, modes of expression
have changed according to the current stage of
technical representation. In the '60s, the transistor,
combined with the stereo effect, gave rise to the
amplified extravagances that broke new ground
in the field of music. It become the dream of a
generation to do just what the Beatles had done:
»rock 'n' roll I gave you all the best years of my
life«. Up until the '70s, this craze for music
involving guitar, bass and drums was confined to
beat-up basement rehearsal studios.

The '80s saw a breakthrough in computer and
video technology together with a multitude of
new television channels. With yet another form
of technology, the Internet, our age is becoming
an increasingly vision-based one. Now, as in the
middle ages, a great deal of information is being
communicated in pictorial or symbolic format
causing cultural doom-mongers to eagerly predict
an immanent return to illiteracy.

The screen designer can adapt to the visualisation
of our environment and, in so doing, get round
the low-quality presentation of text. Texts are,
wherever possible, worded as precise summaries
and broken down into short segments. A consideration here is exactly how the eyes will scan from

the heading through to the actual body of the
text. Thus, rather than being relayed by the text,
information can be communicated by means of
colours and colour contrasts.

Extreme type styles such as condensed, in particular, ultracondensed as well as very bold ought not to be used on the screen: they can often only be presented in a distorted form (condensed) or tend to clump together (bold). Factors influencing this are type size and the colour contrast of the text to background.

»Letters are things
and not pictures of things.«
Eric Gill

Bodoni

Helvetica 25

Helvetica 35

Helvetica 45

Helvetica 55

Bodoni

Helvetica 25

Helvetica 35

Helvetica 45

Helvetica 55

Bodoni

Helvetica 25

Helvetica 35

Helvetica 45

Helvetica 55

1.1 **Thin and normal type styles in 40 pt.**

1.2 **Thin and normal type styles in 12 pt.**

Thin, normal, semi-bold and bold styles

Bodoni

(on paper)

Bodoni

1.1.1 **(on screen)**

Helvetica 25

Helvetica 35

1.1.2

1.1.1
It can clearly be seen how the fine lines of Bodoni are made to fit into the coarseness of the pixel grid.
1.1.2
The same is evident for the ultra-thin style Helvetica.
(enlarged)

Parameters such as type size and contrast between text and background determine, to a large degree, the precision with which the text is represented together with its finer details.

If the text is too small, it can completely disintegrate into pixels so that the finer lines don't always correspond exactly to the pixel grid of the screen: it may be the case that the finer lines disappear altogether or artificially spill over into a pixel row. The result is an unpleasant and seemingly formless jumble of letters, bearing little or no resemblence to a well designed text (1.1.1). The same is true of all the thin styles, which, when seen on the screen as part of a text, are often impossible to distinguish from one another (1.1.2). If this is further complicated by the text being set against a light-coloured or white background, excessive brightness from the background can further limit the readability of the text (1.2).
The designer is therefore better off not using thin styles at all, unless the type size is set very high: upwards of 40 pt (1.1).

Normal styles are generally very well suited to the screen, as long as the minimum size is at least 12 pt. Nonetheless, the use of any font or style should be individually weighed up both in terms of suitability on screen and with consideration to the interplay between colour and background – the excessive brightness emitted by a very light-coloured or white background causes normal styles to seem slightly smaller compared to light-coloured text on a dark background.

For texts in bold, the general rule of thumb is: the bolder the style, the greater the letter spacing (or tracking) needs to be (2.1). This applies especially to smaller-sized type, which can otherwise clump together. As with the extreme forms of thin styles such as »ultra light«, the use of bold styles is, for the reasons outlined above, not advised. In addition to this, the technical requirements cannot offer such precise typographical manipulation and thus the letter spacing (tracking) has to be stored as an image.

With logos and other labels of a fixed nature that repeat themselves and don't have to be read, but rather noticed and recognised, composition using extreme styles is practical – this becomes less applicable as a mode of emphasis in texts since the type size is too small for typographic details of this nature.

Synonyms | Line Thickness

2 extrathin, ultra light

3 thin

4 light

5 normal, book, regular, roman

6 medium, semibold

7 bold

8 extrabold, heavy

9 black

Helvetica 65	Helvetica 65 +10
Helvetica 75	Helvetica 75 +10
Helvetica 85	Helvetica 85 +15
Helvetica 95	Helvetica 95 +15

2.1 **Bold styles in 12 pt.**
Left, without incresed letter spacing (tracking).
Right, with increased letter spacing (tracking).

2 Helvetica 25 Ultra Light 10 pt
Helvetica 25 Ultra Light 12 pt

3 Helvetica 35 Thin 10 pt
Helvetica 35 Thin 12 pt

4 Helvetica 45 Light 10 pt
Helvetica 45 Light 12 pt

5 Helvetica 55 Normal 10 pt
Helvetica 55 Normal 12 pt

6 Helvetica 65 Medium 10 pt
Helvetica 65 Medium 12 pt

7 Helvetica 75 Bold 10 pt
Helvetica 75 Bold 12 pt

8 Helvetica 85 Heavy 10 pt
Helvetica 85 Heavy 12 pt

9 Helvetica 95 Black 10 pt
Helvetica 95 Black 12 pt

2.04

058.059

Type styles:
letter spacing
line slopes

Traditional typography has a large number of options that either don't function on the screen at all, or only do so to a limited extent. Included among these are italics and finer styles, which should where possible be avoided.

»When designing type for the Web,
I don't think much like a typographer.
I think like a guy giving a drunken fratboy directions
to the International House of Pancakes at 4a.m.«
Eric Eaton

2.1–3.3
Type styles in the pixel grid: normal, bold and italic.

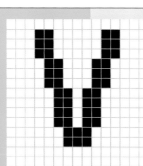 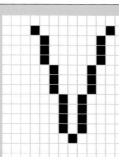 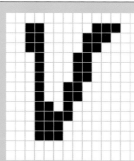 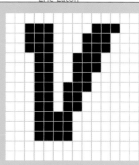

2.1 **Helvetica Normal** 2.2 **Helvetica Light** 2.3 **Helvetica Normal Italic** 2.4 **Helvetica Bold Italic**

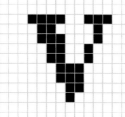 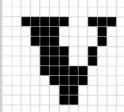 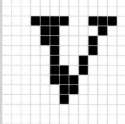

3.1 **Times** 3.2 **Times Bold** 3.3 **Times Italic**

TANITH   dates : foren

Condensed, extended and italic styles

Times
T T
m m

1.1
More than one style of italics: Shown here in black is the Times typeface artificially altered to give an italic style.
In white is the Times italic style as taken from the font menu —— far better suited to the screen because it doesn't slope quite as much as the artificial variety and because the form of the serifs and the course followed by the lines is less forced.

Even on paper – an ideal background because of its high levels of resolution – an italic style used for large sections of text makes reading difficult. A characteristic of italic styles is the sloping typeface and it is precisely this that makes it so difficult to read, the problem being that diagonals are represented as steps on the screen. These steps, arising in the pixelisation, cause the text to appear very messy (**2.1–3.3**). The quality of italics is improved – albeit only to a small degree – by increasing the size of the type, therefore this style should really only be used very sparingly or, better still, left out altogether.

With texts on the screen, much depends on whether they are represented as a graphic or as normal text. With graphics, there are far more possibilities open to the screen designer for presenting and differentiating between type styles: there is, for example, more than one style of italics (**1.1**). The designer is able to select a more suitable style from a menu – the downside is that this may increase the time needed for loading.

Condensed styles are similarly best avoided, in particular compressed italic styles and condensed finer styles. Such combinations

result in unharmonious-looking clumps of letters or letters which, due to the formation of steps and the inconvenience of each line not corresponding exactly to a pixel, lose their appeal for the reader (**2.3**, **2.4**).
Extended styles and bold styles (**4.1**) are best incorporated only in conjunction with wide spacing, otherwise there is a danger – particularly with smaller type sizes – of letters clumping together. If the aim is to present an elegant-looking, highly readable text, extended and italic styles are just as inadvisable on the screen as they are on paper.

in a working environment which is highly stimulating, because at Northwind every project is above

Bernhard Lassahn

für die grossen

für die grossen

Italic and compressed styles are not really suitable as modes of emphasis for the screen. As an alternative, variations in text colour may be used or, where a

subtler effect is required, the text colour simply applied at a reduced tone.

Synonyms | Letter spacing and line slopes

2 extra expanded, extra extended

3 expanded, extended

4 extended italic, extended oblique

5 normal, regular

6 normal italic, normal oblique

7 condensed, compressed, narrow

8 condensed italic, condensed oblique

9 extra condensed

Blur

Blur

iwitness

iwitness

left:
Italic styles and line slopes are used here only as logos and represented on a large enough scale so that an appearance of relative neatness is maintained.

sting Services from
Lower Total Cost of

left:
A badly chosen colour contrast can drastically reduce the readability of italic and bold styles.

4.1
Bold and extended styles work well on screen – provided the type size is not too small.

W/Brasil, Brazil's best-known and third-largest agency,

e : charts : texte : pics : links : shop

2 Helvetica 23 Ultra Light Extended
Helvetica 24 Ultra Light Extended Italic
Helvetica 25 Ultra Light
Helvetica 26 Ultra Light Italic
Helvetica 27 Ultra Light Condensed
Helvetica 28 Ultra Light Condensed Italic

3 Helvetica 33 Thin Extended
Helvetica 34 Thin Extended Italic
Helvetica 35 Thin
Helvetica 36 Thin Italic
Helvetica 37 Thin Condensed
Helvetica 38 Thin Condensed Italic

4 Helvetica 43 Light Extended
Helvetica 44 Light Extended Italic
Helvetica 45 Light
Helvetica 46 Light Italic
Helvetica 47 Light Condensed
Helvetica 48 Light Condensed Italic

5 Helvetica 53 Extended
Helvetica 54 Extended Italic
Helvetica 55 Normal
Helvetica 56 Normal Italic
Helvetica 57 Condensed
Helvetica 58 Condensed Italic

6 Helvetica 63 Medium Extended
Helvetica 64 Medium Extended Italic
Helvetica 65 Medium
Helvetica 66 Medium Italic
Helvetica 67 Medium Condensed
Helvetica 68 Medium Condensed Italic

7 **Helvetica 73 Bold Extended**
Helvetica 74 Bold Extended Italic
Helvetica 75 Bold
Helvetica 76 Bold Italic
Helvetica 77 Bold Condensed
Helvetica 78 Bold Condensed Italic

9 **Helvetica 93 Black Extended**
Helvetica 94 Black Extended Italic
Helvetica 95 Black
Helvetica 96 Black Italic
Helvetica 97 Black Compressed
Helvetica 98 Black Compressed Italic

8 **Helvetica 83 Heavy Extended**
Helvetica 84 Heavy Extended Italic
Helvetica 85 Heavy
Helvetica 86 Heavy Italic
Helvetica 87 Heavy Condensed
Helvetica 88 Heavy Condensed Italic

Used on the screen, script styles and experimental fonts can make reading awkward. Their suitability should be checked carefully in each case but it may be better to leave them out since there is a large margin for error. Modes of emphasis such as colour work well while underlining is best left out – again decisions have to be taken according to the situation.

»A great many people have never yet set eyes on a well-formed typeface.«
Jan Tschichold

1.1 **shadow** 2.1 **outlines** 3.1 **underlined**

**Modes of emphasis:
Experimental fonts and
script typefaces**

Poor resolution means that many modes of emphasis are unsuited to use on the screen:

Shadowing
Particularly with smaller font sizes, the shadow can fuse with the background and text, making the word difficult for the eye to grasp (**1.1**).

Outlines
In the worst cases, the fine lines slice through the outer contours and the type becomes distorted to the point of unreadability or, worse still, the fine lines are not represented at all (**2.1**).

Underlining
This is best not used as a mode of emphasis on the screen! Underlined words on screen are used to represent link-options:
click here! (**3.1**).

Kerning
Kerning requires some delicacy. The standard programming format for websites recognises only coarse kerning. The coarse variety can conflict with the line spacing so that the eye has difficulty smoothly scanning a line.

For graphics, the full range of refining techniques is viable – there can however be problems with incorporating these into the flow of the text (**4.1**).

SMALL CAPS
With small caps, two inconveniences are evident: first, the reduced size of the text, and second, that the type is in upper case, something which means the visual form of the word or »word picture« is no longer recognisable at a glance (**5.1**).

Modes of emphasis that create good effects on the screen provided consideration is given to negative factors:

UPPER CASE
If the sections to be highlighted are not too long, i.e. a few words, upper case is well suited. If the passages are too long, the visual form of the words or »word picture« becomes more difficult for the reader to recognise due to the change in typeface (**6.1**).

As vice chairman and
has the responsibility
encouraging creative

eative officer for Leo Burnett Worldwide, Michael Conrad
seeing the agency's global creative product. Provoking and
round the globe, Michael continually challenges Burnett's
7.1 ces to strive toward setting new standards in advertising

As a mode of emphasis, colour tends to work very well: colour changes, if made in a screen-friendly font, produce clear high-lighting that is better than, say, small caps, italics or underlining. By adjusting the strength of the colour contrast, the intensity of the highlight can be determined. Care must still be taken to ensure that the colour used for emphasis forms an acceptable contrast with the background, as indeed should the main text.

TRANS-MEDIA SOMETHING ARTIFACTS ASSERTIONS
FROM
NOTHING   COLOR, FINISHES

6.1   ENVIRONMENTAL

Remedy Double

Sand

Pompeia Inline

OUCH

MOJO

Khaki Two

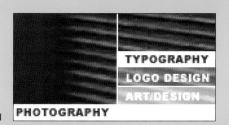

TYPOGRAPHY
LOGO DESIGN
ART/DESIGN
8.1 PHOTOGRAPHY

PREPARATORY WORKSHOPS

4.1 w i d e s p a c e   5.1 SMALL CAPS

W e l c o m e

Colour
Passages of text highlighted in colour are a good form of variance provided the brightness of the highlighted words is sufficient to set them off against the background. Otherwise the effect is reversed and the word or phrase dissolves into the background (**7.**1).

Background
The positioning of text on a coloured background, say, on a block of colour, can result in good effects provided the colours are clearly defined in relation to one another (**8.**1).

Font and type styles
Italics, condensed and narrow styles are not especially well suited, while extended and bold styles tend to work well as modes of emphasis on the screen unless an extreme style, say ultra bold, is used.

Experimental fonts and script styles
Script styles and experimental fonts act much like italics when used on the screen: as with italics, script styles often don't fit into the pixel grid of the screen due to their obliqueness and wide variations in line strength. This causes them to appear messy and illegible. It is appropriate to use them after careful consideration, say for logos or as an eye-catcher, provided they are used in a large enough format.

Particularly with small and bold fonts, the introduction of spacing between letters can make the text easier to read on the screen.

With some font designs, smaller typeface sizes can hardly be read at all on the screen without the introduction of letter spacing.

This text is set in Times, 14 pt with no character spacing.

Times | 14 pt

This text is set in Times, 14 pt with a character spacing set to +5.

Times | 14 pt | +5

This text is set in Times, 14 pt with a character spacing set to +10.

Times | 14 pt | +10

This text is set in Times bold, 10 pt with no character spacing.

Times bold | 10 pt

This text is set in Times bold, 10 pt with a character spacing set to +5.

Times bold | 10 pt | +5

This text is set in Times bold, 10 pt with a character spacing set to +10.

Times bold | 10 pt | +10

Tracking The letter spacing over the line should be sufficient to give the text an even colour, because dark areas where letters bunch together are particularly noticeable in text viewed on screen. If two letters are too close together there is also a danger that they can look like another letter.

This applies particularly for small font sizes and bold fonts. Large fonts need less spacing: there is therefore no proportionality between the spacing and the font size.

Even with modest spacing between letters here they are still difficult to keep apart.

Very wide letter spacing can also be used occasionally as an eye-catcher.

Letter spacing must be used with care, because if the gaps between letters are too large then the words seem to fall apart and instead of being easier to read, the text can actually become even more difficult to read.

w i d e s p a c i n g c a n m a k e a t e x t h a r d t o r e a d .

The spacing needed between letters also depends very much on the spacing between the lines. The distance between the letters should always be smaller than the inter-linear spacing, so that each line retains its horizontal integrity.

This text is set in Helvetica, 14 pt with no character spacing.

Helvetica | 14 pt

This text is set in Helvetica, 14 pt with a character spacing set to +5.

Helvetica | 14 pt | +5

This text is set in Helvetica, 14 pt with a character spacing set to +10.

Helvetica | 14 pt | +10

This text is set in Helvetica bold, 10 pt with no character spacing.

Helvetica bold | 10 pt

This text is set in Helvetica bold, 10 pt with a character spacing set to +5.

Helvetica bold | 10 pt | +5

This text is set in Helvetica bold, 10 pt with a character spacing set to +10.

Helvetica bold | 10 pt | +10

ith a character spacing +5

with no character spacing

with a character spacing +10

typography

typography

t ypography

nwanted ligatures, when letters seem tied together, an result if a very small typeface size is used, or a bold nt design. In such cases, letter spacing should be ded.

Tracking is important if the screen background is dark in comparison with the letters. The bright light from the letters seems to spread over the »dead« screen so that the letters lose resolution, and will merge into one another if set too close together.

m cl co d m cl co d

Leading

Additional leading between lines to about 150% of the compressed typeface size can improve the legibility on screen considerably.

»...the best user interfaces are the result of a combination of sensory richness and machine intelligence.«
Nicholas Negroponte

Wallpaper* uses no inter-linear spacing on its site: the words touch each other and create a sculptural impression. This works with individual words, or when, as here, the words are separated by shades of colour.

Leading The line spacing is a further important parameter when it comes to making texts easier to read on screen.

Most DTP programs have a default setting for line spacing of 120% (where 100% is when the tops of one row of characters would touch the base of the row above). This produces good results for printed texts, but is not sufficient for the presentation of texts on screen; the spacing between lines should be larger than on paper. Interlinear spacing for texts on screen should be 150% or even more.

Here again the rule is: the longer the lines are, then the wider spaced they should be. Wider, lighter fonts need more spacing between lines than narrow, heavier fonts.

If the interlinear spacing is too great then the space between the lines dominates rather than the text, and the eye finds it hard to find the way back to the start of the next line.

Paper: Type size 14 pt | interlinear spacing 120% (default) = 16
(Here on the right, the interlinear spacing which produces a ver result on paper has been transferred to the screen. But the lar interlinear spacing of 150% is clearly much easier to read on screen.)
Screen: Type size 14 pt | interlinear spacing 150% = 21 pt

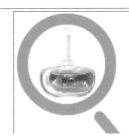

rococo – a modern vision of femininity

expressed through a contemporary interpretation

of the style and spirit of the Rococo period.

180%

A playful reflection of individuality,

self-expression and feminine sensuality.

The spirit of the Rococo period – celebration, opulence, energy

and optimism, a delicate balancing act between reality and illusion.

rococo – a modern reflection of ROCOCO,

a constant source of inspiration to JOOP!

ROCOCO

JOOP!

BACK

ET'S
T SMALL!

s great for Flash, Web and WAP design.

270%

Our bitmap fonts are especially designed for Flash :

they don't blur or fill, and come complete with outl

any print application.

120%

The line spacing is a further important parameter when it comes to making texts easier to read on-screen.
Most DTP programs have a default setting for line spacing of 120% (where 100% is when the tops of one row of characters would touch the base of the row above). This produces good results for printed texts, but is not sufficient for the presentation of texts on screen; the spacing between lines should be larger than on paper.
Interlinear spacing for texts on screen should be 150% or even more.
Here again the rule is: the longer the lines are, then the wider spaced they should be. Wider, lighter fonts need more spacing between lines than narrow, heavier fonts.

150%

The line spacing is a further important parameter when it comes to making texts easier to read on-screen.
Most DTP programs have a default setting for line spacing of 120% (where 100% is when the tops of one row of characters would touch the base of the row above). This produces good results for printed texts, but is not sufficient for the presentation of texts on screen; the spacing between lines should be larger than on paper.

Although the landscape format of the screen makes it very tempting to use long lines of text, it is important that the lines should be kept short.

»Our eyes, due to their fortunate inability to recognise the infinite numbers of small details, only allow that to reach our brain which i[t] must be aware of.«

Eugène Delacroix

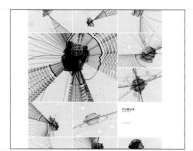

SEMI-AUTOMATIC.

not exactly

KEINE MACHT DER DROGENPOLITIK.

| 10 | 20 | 30 | 40 |

Attributes that can make texts easier to read on screen when used appropriately:
The choice of type
The choice of type size
Tracking
Line length
Interlinear spacing

Line Length

Most screens have a landscape format that seems to invite the use of long lines of text, but in fact it is important to use narrow bodies of text on screen. On paper a column of text can be read comfortably if it is about ten words wide, or 35–55 characters.
But lines on screen should not contain more than 35 characters. The choice of the right line length (column width) is another important criterion along with the choice of typeface and type size when it comes to producing a text that is easy to read on screen. At the same time though, the lines should not be too short, because otherwise it will be necessary to use excessive hyphenation, which makes the text harder to read. The minimum is about 30 characters per line.

The amount of text that can fit on to the page of a book cannot be easily fitted on to the screen in one go if the text is to be legible. Texts on screen should be kept as short as possible.

10   20   30

Lines that can be comfortably read on the screen will usually have about 35 characters per line.

We've also provided you with **more free fonts** plus finally the vector version of Sevenet. A release of the vector version of LipoD will follow next week.

If the lines are long (more than 40 characters) then it is important to choose a larger type size and to use adequate interlinear spacing.

20   30   40   50   60   70   80

Share of Mind.

Zum 1.1.1999 wurde eine Holding gegründet, die die sechs Agenturen verwaltet: die Jung von Matt AG. Sie ist eine geschlossene Aktiengesellschaft. Das Ziel der AG ist, führenden Mitarbeitern die Chance zu geben, am Ergebnis der Agentur zu partizipieren - und ihnen so Verantwortung und Erfolgserlebnis zugleich zu geben. Dennoch ist Shareholder Value nicht das bestimmende Kriterium für Aktien. Für uns

10   20

In the following pages we have selected several projects to show exceptional examples of effective correctly designed lighting. Although we have drawn projects from very different areas, we can only give an indication of the variety of lighting effects here. If you are interested in more specific information, please write to us.

10

14

If lines have less than 30 characters per line then the text (as in this example) should not be too long. The reader will otherwise soon tire of having to jump from one line to the next. Lines should not be presented with an excessively narrow column width because too few characters per line can render a text unreadable. Such a text would involve too many word-breaks and the flow of reading would be greatly limited.

2.08

Text quantity

068.069

In order to make text on the screen as accessible as possible, the lines must not be too long and there must not be too many lines. The best thing is to be as concise as possible.

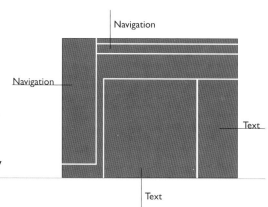

Navigation

Navigation

Text

Text

The text area will rarely cover the entire screen. There will normally be a navigation bar at the top of the screen or down the left-hand side, and the available area is correspondingly smaller. On the Gucci page the visitor can read a longer text in the appropriate text window by means of scrolling.

The website of the design school **ESAG** has a navigation bar on the left and text columns aligned next to this.

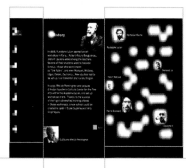

Text

Navigation

Te

Text quantity The landscape format on a screen has the advantage over typical printed pages that short text blocks (not more than 25 lines) can be distributed in many ways. Text can be presented in a number of columns across the screen, which offers an element of flexibility.

The texts should be as concise as possible, and the contents should preferably be divided up so that it can be presented in short blocks. If the text is in 12 point (and on screen texts should never be smaller) and the lines have 35 characters, there is room for three parallel columns on a screen, with space left over for a navigation bar.

The Internet is seen as a »fast« medium. That affects the way people approach reading on-line: The texts should be short and to the point.

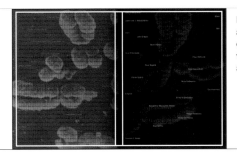

In the production of books and print products the designer only has to do without text in the margins and on the binding.

The website of **NASA20** uses dynamic text and navigation boxes. The information appears in separate windows.

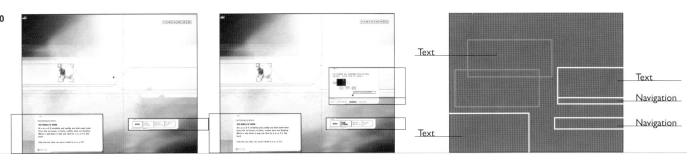

Text

Text

Navigation

Text

Navigation

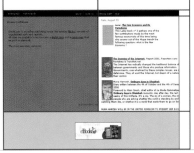

On the website of **00h00** publishers, the navigation bars are situated at the top and bottom of the screen. The text is distributed between two windows, in one of which the text can be scrolled.

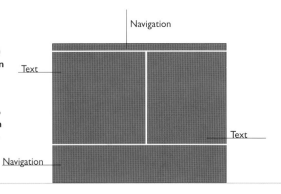

Navigation

Text

Text

Navigation

The designer of a website should take into account that there are areas on the screen that will not be included on a print-out. If a page is intended to be printed then extra margins should be included so that none of the text or images are lost.

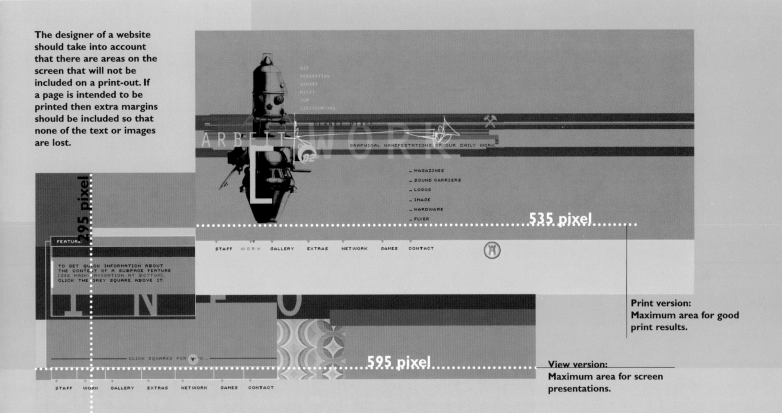

295 pixel

535 pixel

595 pixel

Print version:
Maximum area for good print results.

View version:
Maximum area for screen presentations.

If all the rules of classic typography are modified to
suit the poor resolution of the digital interface, then
the resultant text is easy to read.

»...a society in which they wear coloured watches,
in a society like this I am only in the way,
digital is better, digital is better for me.«
tocotronic

A larger typeface than would usually be used for text
on paper helps to make it easier to understand information presented on the monitor screen.

The main horizontal and vertical strokes of a font
should, ideally, align perfectly with the pixel grid.
If the strokes are thinner than one pixel, which they
obviously can't be, so the characters vary: The letter
»l« shows what happens when a stroke misses the natural grid. The first »l« is spread across two pixels but in
the second it is perfectly formed.

Club has to close down soon?

No, definitely not for the time being, but because of it
proximity to Potsdamer Platz, the area is now well-
known as the most expensive undeveloped real esta
in Berlin. But we've always been aware that an end
would come to the wild parties in "the vault". The own
of the property Tresor Club now stands on has alrea
written the Federal Republic of Germany's Office of
State Lands several times regarding the sale of the
area. As far as we know, no new owner has come fo
yet. Luckily for us, the land the club sits on isn't very
cheap and has a major subway line directly beneath
as well, so if someone could actually afford buying th

Your questions:

Will Tresor close down soon?
Check out my music demo...
Tickets
Flyers
Tresor posters or stickers
Tresor News
If I'm not 18-years-old...
Rent the Tresor Club...
Is the Tresor 100 years old?

News faq

Frequently Asked Questions

Is it true that Tresor Club has to close down soon?

No, definitely not for the time being, but because of its
proximity to Potsdamer Platz, the area is now well-
known as the most expensive undeveloped real estate
in Berlin. But we've always been aware that an end
would come to the wild parties in "the vault". The owner
of the property Tresor Club now stands on has already
written the Federal Republic of Germany's Office of
State Lands several times regarding the sale of the
area. As far as we know, no new owner has come forth
yet. Luckily for us, the land the club sits on isn't very
cheap and has a major subway line directly beneath it
as well, so if someone could actually afford buying the
land, there's little chance that any large new buildings

NET SHOP CONTACT GUIDE

Tresor. news   Love Parade   On Tour   FAQ   Guestbook   SMS

It's Time To Party Wild!

Tresor.core

▶ **Each Friday**
  Hardcore, Gabba, Techno, Noize

▶ **Club.program**

Club special

Tresor.core   german |

Each Friday: Hardcore, Gabba, Techno, Noize

Though Tresor in 1991 was the first club, which also played the hardest kind of
Techno, we have somewhat lost the development of Hardcore Techno through
the years. Nowadays Techno isn't only underground at all and so many people
us, "Techno is out", which is of course as true as HipHop and Rock are also ou

But, there is still the search for new thrills. There is a tendency for harder, rough
sounds in recent times, artists like Neil Landstrumm or Cristian Vogel use the
power and rawness from the punk era. It's time for Hardcore again. Back to da
roots, without any pathetic "good old days".

The Hardcore scene is still quite alive, it is well organised and there is an
impressive community worldwide. The only thing missing in Berlin is a club as
home base for the Hardcore scene. We like to change this, from now on; new

Program
Special
Booking
Love Parade
Video
History

NEWS SHOP CONTACT GUIDE

Tresor. net   Club

Tresor. net   Club   Label   Network   Roots   M

**Good typography is just as important on a Web page as
it is in any other medium. The fact that it appears on a
computer screen and not on a piece of paper is imma-
terial, it should still be pleasing to look at and easy to
read: Grotesque typefaces provide a clean appearance.**

**A typeface which is harmonised with the backg
makes the text easy to read. If the colour is too
glaring or the contrast is too great then the ove
impression can be fuzzy, and the text is difficult
to read.**

Information is provided piece by piece, so that the reader finds it easier to absorb the message, despite the poor screen resolution.

Texts on screen set in grotesque typefaces work very well on the screen as large and bold types.

3

**What are the viable ways of improving
readability on screen?
To what extent can symbols, icons and digital
assistants be used to replace text?**

3.01

074.**075**

Developments

Writing tools have always had a definitive influence
on the writing itself.
To what extent has the computer influenced the
development of today's typefacing?

»Keep going,
going on, call that going,
call that on.«
Samuel Beckett

Greek clay-tablet writing
around 200 B.C.

Egyptian hieroglyphics
Pictorial writing system,
around 3000 B.C.

Phoenician
Pictorial system of signs,
around 1500 B.C.

**Phoenician consonantal
writing system**
Pictorial writing system,
around 1200 B.C.

Ancient Greek
around 900 B.C.

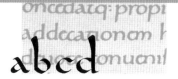

**Gutenberg invents
printing using
moveable letters**
around 1445.

**Since Gutenberg,
the development of
text has accelerated.**

Halbunziale
around A.D. 500

National script
around A.D. 700

Carolingian Minuscule
around A.D. 900

Textur, Rotunda, Schwabacher
around A.D. 1400–1500

Developments
The development of writing has not only been
determined by the materials on which the writing
appears – i.e. clay tablet and paper – but also by
the corresponding tools that render the writing
readable, i.e. chisel, quill and ink or printing
machine. Fine lines, for example, first became
possible with the introduction of copperplate
engraving. If one makes a comparison between
the many ways of presenting text – each of
which has shown a tendency to develop towards
fineness – and the results on screen, the coarseness of today's text representation on a computer
seems almost backward.

Does that mean that we are living through a
decisive phase in the development of writing in
which we are seeing a reverse (or regressive)
development back towards the pictorial symbol?
For one thing, that would mean national languages
no longer playing such a key role in the worldwide network. Or will the screen's representation
and resolution improve? Even if the resolution
were to become more refined, the fact remains
that in comparison with paper, on which writing
is materially represented, text on the screen is
created through the use of light – the way of
doing things is different and the text itself also

undergoes a change. Which tool is available today
to help render rudimentary text in the most
asthetic way possible?

ΛBCD

ΛϐϾⅅ

ʌ

ΛBCO

Monumentalis script gave rise to Rustica and, later, italics, both of which were suited to the brisk strokes of the quill and ink pen.

Unziale script, written with the quill held at an almost horizontal angle, arose from the need for faster systems of writing.

Serifs were probably a by-product of the chisel technique.

Roman Capitalis Monumentalis
around A.D. 200

Roman Capitalis Quadrata
Pictorial writing system, around A.D. 400

Roman Capitalis Rustica
around A.D. 400

Roman italics

Unziale
around A.D. 500

Aabcd

Aabcd
ABCD
Aabcd

Aabcd
Aabcd

Aabcd
Aabcd

Renaissance-Antiqua
about A.D. 1500

Linear-Antiqua
about A.D. 1900

Diversity of writing styles
after 1945

Writing on the screen
2003

Human beings have always had visions of the future and strived for a better world:
Of utmost urgency in today's world is a vision for the improvement of poor quality text representation on the computer!

»[...] Should I mention
before going any further,
any further on,
that I say a priori,
without knowing what it means.«
Samuel Beckett

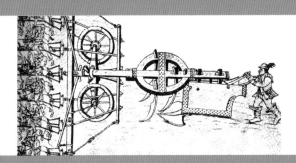

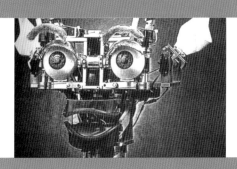

Future visions and human striving:
Top of page:
»What do we want to say to a being from another planet?«
Far left:
Plough monstrosity with giant ploughshare, end of the 16th century.
Left:
Robots »Robo Sapiens«.

3.02

Standards

Even if levels of resolution were vastly improved, any representation on the screen would still be composed of light. Due to the intensive contrasts and the idiosyncratic way of composing images, restrictions on readability will surely always remain a factor.

»Human beings and their environment form a networked system. When acting as the protagonist at any one point, one must also be prepared for changes to occur at another point.
H. W. Franke

A pixel is best thought of as a tiny point in the form of a square.

Yet the perceived effect is that of a fuzzy dot.

The white pixel is in fact an illusion – it is made up of thin red, green and blue lines:
Each point of colour on the screen is the sum of the (red, green and blue – RGB) light emitted by the three cathodes comprising the cathode ray tube.

1.1 Representation by aperture grill.
1.2 Representation by shadow mask.

On an LCD (Liquid Crystal Display) screen, the electronic dot is represented by means of crystals.

What are the causes of bad readability on screen?

1.1 aperture grill

1.2 shadow mask

Monitor technology
CTR Cathode Ray Tube
The CTR principle relies on three electron canons, each corresponding to one of the primary colours of the additive colour system (red, green, blue) and responsible for producing a ray of electrons. Through an electronic process, this ray is catapulted on to a glass plate coated with phosphor, which as a result begins to glow. What we see on the screen is the product of the three primary colours of the additive colour model (RGB), mixed at varying levels of intensity with the result that a broad range of colours is represented. Instead of perceiving three individual points of colour, our eye sees a single pixel. Before the electrons hit the phosphor coating, they must pass through a mask – this bundles the electrons. The mask, which splits up the light, is either an aperture grill or a shadow mask. The aperture grill has square-shaped holes and can let through more light than the shadow mask, which is composed of circular holes. With both varieties, a proportion of the light gets absorbed and consequently the monitor is unable to represent the pure white that would result from the mixture of RGB. Neither is the representation of pitch black quite so straightforward since this is

hindered by light reflecting off the glass plate. The shorter the distance separating the holes (i.e. the lower the pitch), the finer the representation formed by dots and pixels on the screen. In order to achieve a dpi (dots per inch) of say 72 on the sceen, it is necessary to have a dot pitch of 0.28mm. Most displays sold today have a dot pitch of between 0.2mm and 0.3mm, which explains why type can only be very coarsely represented on the screen – the technology on offer today just won't allow higher levels of resolution, at least not at prices that are affordable. The interface which finally channels the visual output of data is the graphics card. Linked up to this is the display, which has the job of representing the signals as an image on the monitor. The display unit determines the on-screen output and, as such, is responsible for resolution, refresh rate, range of colours and the speed at which graphics are built up on the screen. Even if, as experts claim, resolution on the screen will one day be just as good as that of paper, other problems will still remain to be solved – the representation of images will still be composed of light, thus necessitating a completely different approach.

Monitor sizes (diagonal measurement) with
recommended levels of resolution

14-inch screen	640 x	480	pixels
15-inch screen	800 x	600	pixels
17-inch screen	832 x	624	pixels
19-inch screen	1024 x	768	pixels
20-inch screen	1152 x	870	pixels
22-inch screen	1280 x	1024	pixels

The resolution of the
screen is an all-important
factor in the represen-
tation of diagonals and
curves: the higher the
resolution offered, the
less evident the »step
effect«.

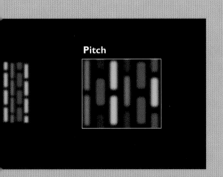

Pitch

**The distance separating
the holes of the shadow
mask is known as the
pitch and determines
the display's resolution.**

**A sketch for the
Telectroscope by
Constantin Senlecq,
dating 1880.**

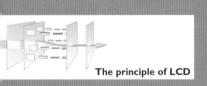

The principle of LCD

LCD-Displays

Liquid Crystal Display or LCD is the term used
to refer to screens based on liquid crystal technology. Through electrical impulses, the liquid crystal
can be made to change its alignment so that light
coming from a unit behind the screen either
shines through or is blocked out. How much
light is let through and which colours result, is
determined by the polarisation filter, the colour
filter and two alignment layers. In dots of red,
green and blue, the light then hits precisely the
area represented by a pixel.

This technology, while eliminating screen flicker,
is of no advantage as far as the eyesore of the
pixel is concerned – here, too, higher resolution
would still come at a higher cost.

A further factor which plays an important role
in the effective representation of information
on screen is the refresh rate.

The refresh rate refers to the number of times
per second the image displayed on screen can
be redrawn – the higher the refresh rate, the
smoother the picture appears to be. The lower
the refresh rate, the more the screen will flicker.
For refresh rates of 72 Hertz (Hz) per second
and above, the eye no longer perceives any flicker.

3.02

Standards

There are two principles by which type can be displayed
on the screen: as vector type or as bitmap type.

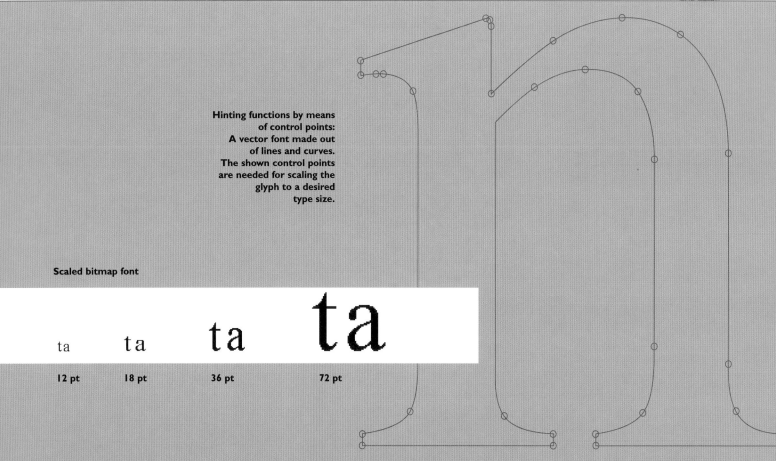

**Hinting functions by means
of control points:
A vector font made out
of lines and curves.
The shown control points
are needed for scaling the
glyph to a desired
type size.**

Scaled bitmap font

ta   ta   ta   ta

12 pt   18 pt   36 pt   72 pt

Vector or bitmap type? Type may be saved to disc in one of two
formats – either as vector or as bitmap.
Bitmap type is stored together with specifica-
tions for the visual impact of pixel points. These
pixel points carry information regarding colour
which is either just black or just white, plus
additional data concerning shades of grey and
colour. Vector type is composed of »outlines«,
generated by bézier curves or splines. The
advantage of this variety is that it enables the
easy reduction or enlargement of type by scaling, with the added bonus that large representations don't take up much memory.

Unscaled bitmap type can really deliver great
effects on screen, yet as soon as it is scaled,
the quality rapidly deteriorates. In order to
ensure good representation, type sizes have to
be individually stored, which – especially where
very large sizes are concerned – can take up a
lot of memory. It follows then, that vector type
is better suited for large scale representations
while, where small-scale representation is
required, it is preferable to use bitmap type.
In order that outlines and vectors, originally
designed for print format, be made practical

for use on screen, they need to undergo a
hinting process. This procedure maps the
contours of the letters on to the pixel grid
and optimises represention on screen
(above right).

PACK MY BOX
THE LAZY DOG
WYVERN FOXY
pack my box with

PACK MY BOX
THE LAZY DOG
WYVERN FOXY
pack my box

Far left:
Uneven spacing in a short text sample.
(Enlarged)

Left:
**Even spacing. Each letter spaces well and the effect is a well suitable text.
(True Type Font)**
(Enlarged)

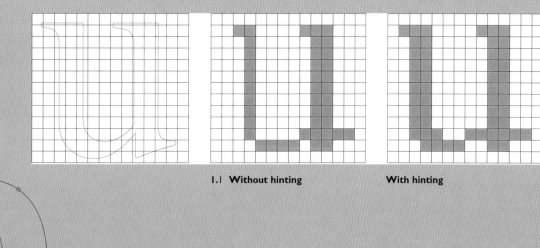

1.1 **Without hinting**   **With hinting**

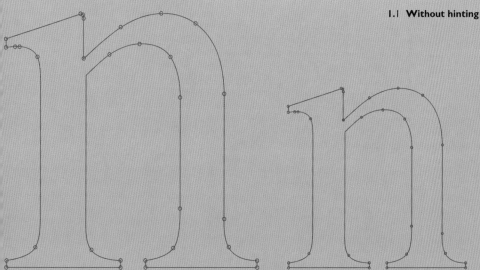

Hinting
True Type
PostScript
Type 1 Fonts

True Type fonts are identifiable by the data suffix »ttf« or by the True Type symbol.

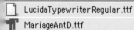

LucidaTypewriterRegular.ttf
MariageAntD.ttf

As long as hardware solutions to tackle the problem of low resolution on screen remain unavailable, software solutions will still be required to remedy, or at least partly alleviate, the inadequate representation offered by low-resolution displays.

The fact that pixels are of a restricted size, can lead to irregularities arising in the final representation of the letters.

Small type sizes are especially prone to unappealing blockiness since the form of the letter does not always fit into the screen's grid (1.1).

With anti-aliasing, the computer is able to convert irregularities into grey shade.

Hinting, on the other hand, is a mathematical modification of text on the screen. It ensures uniformity of positioning and spacing, influencing proportion and thereby affecting the overall appearance of the text. Hinting is the best possible method of presenting small type sizes at low resolution since, for the most part, it retains the characteristics typical of the various fonts. Software stored on the computer's hard disk recognises familiar and reoccu-

ring components of the letters such as line thickness, form elements and serifs. For each component recognised, the software produces a version corresponding to the type format in question (True Type or PostScript Type 1 Fonts) with the result that letters of varying type size are given an appearence of uniformity and the contours optimised for the grid matrix. This goes a long way towards improving readability and pattern recognition of text on the screen. With the type formats mentioned here – True Type or PostScript Type 1 Fonts – a letter is not prepared as a pixel grid, but rather defined as a vector which can then be scaled accordingly. With hinting, this is different: Control points of some sort or another are set by the program's manufacturer, similar to those of the True Type and PostScript methods. The right kind of hints can save a lot of work, which is why caution should be observed when typefaces of this nature are offered at low prices.

3.03

Improvements
Anti-aliasing

Smooth finishing on text gives the letters a less jagged, more readable feel but also reduces the sharpness of the contours.

»Once entangled in communication,
one can never return to the paradise of the simple souls agai
(not even, as Kleist hoped, through the backdoor).«
Niklas Luhmann

Times, anti-aliased, »sharp«
Helvetica, anti-aliased, »sharp«

solar wolves

1.1 **Helvetica, 18 pt on paper**

Times, anti-aliased, »sharp«
Helvetica, anti-aliased, »sharp«

solar wolves

1.2 **Helvetica, 18 pt on paper**

Times, anti-aliased, »strong«
Helvetica, anti-aliased, »strong«

solar wolves

2.1 **Helvetica, not anti-aliased, 18 pt on screen**

Times, anti-aliased, »strong«
Helvetica, anti-aliased, »strong«

solar wolves

2.2 **Helvetica, not anti-aliased, 18 pt on screen**

Times, anti-aliased, »smooth«
Helvetica, anti-aliased, »smooth«

Times, anti-aliased, »smooth«
Helvetica, anti-aliased, »smooth«

Anti-aliasing

The jagged effects that result when texts are presented on current-day monitor screens can be smoothed out by a process known as »anti-aliasing« to produce texts that are easier to read. The pixels of the font seem smoother and more highly resolved.
Anti-aliasing on screen results in the jagged edges on diagonal and curved lines being filled in with intermediate colours. When magnified many times the result might seem distorted, out of focus, and illegible, but without magnification the contours seem smooth and clear.

The advantage of using screen fonts with anti-aliasing is that on the screen they appear in the font and in the layout that was originally intended in contrast to HTML-texts.
HTML, developed to present texts on the World Wide Web independent of browsers and systems, is often unable to meet design requirements.
In comparison with HTML texts, the disadvantage of anti-aliased text graphics is that alterations or updating is more difficult and time-consuming.

**Anti-aliased text graphics take longer to download and open.
HTML-texts without anti-aliasing appear immediately.**

The examples shown below clearly demonstrate how some letters, particularly those comprising diagonals (v, w) or curved edges (s, o, e, a) may be given a more polished feel through the use of smooth finishing.

With characters comprising verticle or horizontal lines, there is no variation between smooth and normal finishing: these letters do not seem to break down into pixels since their orthogonal forms correspond to the pixel grid (l, i).

Some programs, like ATM (Adobe Type Manager), include a smooth-finishing option, whereby texts on the screen are altered by the operating system.

solar wolves solar wolves

S S (zoomed)

solar wolves solar wolves

S S (zoomed)

solar wolves solar wolves

S S (zoomed)

solar wolves solar wolves

S S (zoomed)

solar wolves solar wolves

S S (zoomed)

solar wolves solar wolves

S S (zoomed)

Without smooth finishing, a text represented on screen appears blocky at the edges (2.1, 2.2) – a stark contrast to the representation on paper (1.1, 1.2).

Selecting the »sharp« setting gives the text a smoother finish while still leaving the edges relatively sharply focused.

The »strong« option liberally attaches the text to the background colour. The letters consequently appear to increase in size slightly.

Examples of anti-aliasing on logos.

TYPOTERROR

VERLAG VORWERK 8

internationales literaturfestival , berlin

3.03

Improvements
Anti-aliasing

It does not necessarily always follow that anti-aliasing improves readability: with some typefaces (bitmaps) and smaller texts, it is better not to use smooth finishing.

»Computer graphics are bringing visual aesthetics into the realm of logic. The logical term »possible worlds«, coined by Leibniz at the end of the 17th century, has become reality. As the poet Musil put it, in the future, we will need to be a great deal more aware of possibilities than of reality.«
Holger van den Boom

Larger font sizes seem clearer on screen when anti-aliasing is used.

Logos should always be loaded as images so that the fonts and the relative font sizes remain unaltered.

Most buttons and navigation elements appear with anti-aliasing as formatted images.

Anti-aliasing   Aliasing is a term used to describe the undesirable effects produced when visual information is presented at a lower than optimal resolution. Anti-aliasing is an excellent function for making typefaces on screen more legible and less cluttered. But it should only be used for larger font sizes. Because when anti-aliasing is used for small font sizes the result is a fuzzy text that can actually be harder to read. Where different font sizes are used on the same page the overall effect can therefore be improved if anti-aliasing is not applied to areas using small font sizes such as menu items.

Anti-aliasing should not be used for font sizes below 14 point, better 18 point.
Specially-designed screen fonts such as New York, Monaco, Geneva or Chicago have a bitmap that is adapted to the screen resolution and already optimised for reading on screen. Anti-aliasing should not be used with bitmap fonts.

6 pt	Not anti-aliased	Anti-aliased
Chicago	solar wolves	solar wolves
Univers	solar wolves	solar wolves
Arial	solar wolves	solar wolves
Times	solar wolves	solar wolves

The enlarged examples show why smooth finishing is best not used with small sized type: the true contours of the letter are lost and it becomes unrecognisibly blurred.

Far left: **Not anti-aliased letter** in a small type size.
Middle: **Anti-aliased letter** in a small type size.
Left: **Anti-aliased letter** in a huge type size.
(All three examples are zoomed in on)

For texts that have to be edited quickly and small typefaces, it is better to use a well designed screen font.

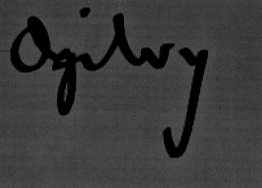

History

INTRODUCTION
TIMELINE
▸ DAVID OGILVY REMEMBERED
BIOGRAPHY
OGILVYISMS
CORPORATE CULTURE
CLASSIC ADS
▸ BOOKS

David Ogilvy (1911-1999)

David Ogilvy said "You will never win fame and fortune unless you invent *big ideas*."

He followed his own advice; Mr. Ogilvy helped establish modern advertising. Among his big ideas: positioning a brand, taking advantage of consumer research, and building a corporate culture.

‹‹ PREVIOUS PAGE | NEXT PAGE ››

For texts that might have to be edited quickly and have a font size of less than 10 point, anti-aliasing should not be used – as seen in this example.

David Ogilvy (1911-1999)

David Ogilvy said "You will never win fame and fortune unless you invent *big ideas*."

He followed his own advice; Mr. Ogilvy helped establish modern advertising. Among his big ideas: positioning a brand, taking advantage of consumer research, and building a corporate culture.

Texts in small sized type become indistinct due to the lack of sharpness created by anti-aliasing and it is preferable not to use smooth finishing.

12 pt	Not anti-aliased	Anti-aliased	18 pt	Not anti-aliased	Anti-aliased
	solar wolves	solar wolves		solar wolves	solar wolves
	solar wolves	solar wolves		solar wolves	solar wolves
	solar wolves	solar wolves		solar wolves	solar wolves
	solar wolves	solar wolves		solar wolves	solar wolves

3.03

Improvements
Colours

Colour resolution as well as colour contrast between text and background can contribute a great deal to readability.
Colour anti-aliasing in a suitable type size can go a long way towards improving readability.

»...What one owns in black and white,
one may comfortably carry home.«
Johann Wolfgang von Goethe

There is no need for white backgrounds: the examples show good results concerning the readability on coloured backgrounds. Be aware of not too strong and not too weak contrasts between the colours of the background and type.

Improvements with colours

The colour resolution (not too low), the type size (not too small) and the colour contrast (not too intensive), can, if chosen with care, vastly improve readabilty.

Colours are a good way of improving readability on the screen. The disadvantages symptomatic of the low resolution of the screen can be balanced out by this kind of advantage, i.e. by making use of colours, which, in contrast to other media, cost nothing when used on the screen. If one were limited to using the black-on-white that we have got so used to seeing in print, it would severely disrupt readability in the electronic format. This much-used scheme – which for the unfortunate reason that we have become accustomed to seeing it, appears far too often on the screen – is about the worst the eyes can be subjected to. The contrast is very strong because the white background is composed of light at its full setting (see page 46).
Anti-aliasing of coloured text and coloured background produces good results if the colour contrasts are chosen with care, the type size is correct and the colour resolution on a low setting (1.1).

1.1

solar wolves

With 16 colours

solar wolves

With 256 colours

solar wolves

With 32,678 colours

The colour resolution for anti-aliasing should neither be too high nor too deep: Too few colours can mean that those used for the text don't combine well with the background, while too many colours will increase the file size of the graphic image. An acceptable representation taking up relatively little memory space is a resolution of 256 colours.

Without anti-aliasing **With anti-aliasing**

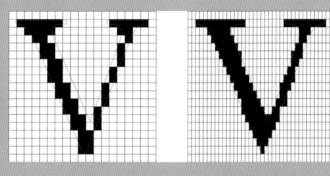

Colour contrasts
Colour anti-aliasing

The colour contrast created between a text and its background plays an important role in the pleasant feel and readability of texts.
The contrasts come across as very intensive due to the light-based composition of the colours. The screen designer can get good results by using a fairly unsaturated background of reduced intrinsic brightness overlayed with light text (see page 46).

Further scope for improving readability is made viable by colour anti-aliasing on LCD-displays, of the sort used in slimline displays, notebooks and e-books. This kind of processing, of which CoolType from Adobe is one example, works using the individual elements of a pixel and not with graded tone values of complete pixels positioned within blocky step formations so as to create an effect of smoothness. With this kind of processing, the primary colours and building blocks of every pixel – red, green and blue (RGB), that also enable the presentation of all the colours on the screen – are used at appropriate points to gloss over any blockiness. The result is smoothly drawn letters that – thanks to the fineness of the pixel elements working to create an optical illusion – appear very sharp but not in the least bit blocky.

3.04

086.**087**

Alternatives:
Symbols and icons

The Internet is a global network. In order to overcome language barriers to its international application, visual markers, pictograms and icons have become important alternatives to text.

»An image says more than a thousand words.«
German saying

Pictogram
[Latin-Greek] synonymous with
Icon [English]
A clear and simple symbolic image that is universally accepted and suitable as a stylised visual means for the conveyance of information. Airports are one example of how pictograms are used. Icons are found as symbols in on-screen graphic interfaces for the visual representation of objects such as hardware apparatus, data files or tasks to be executed by mouse click.

Internationally accepted pictograms may be useful in overcoming the problem of language choice in verbal communication. Script may also take up excessive amounts of limited available space.

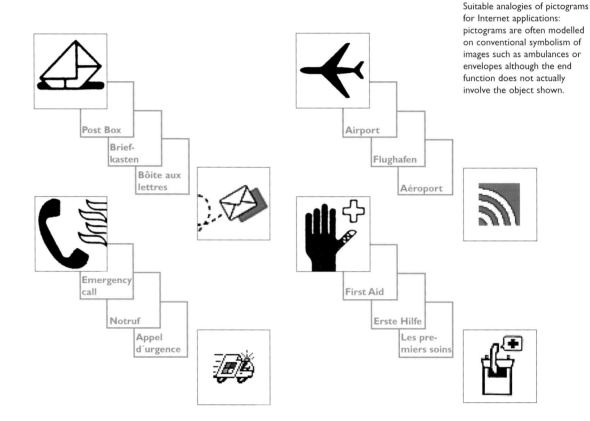

Post Box
Brief-
kasten
Bôite aux
lettres

Emergency
call
Notruf
Appel
d´urgence

Airport
Flughafen
Aéroport

First Aid
Erste Hilfe
Les pre-
miers soins

Suitable analogies of pictograms for Internet applications: pictograms are often modelled on conventional symbolism of images such as ambulances or envelopes although the end function does not actually involve the object shown.

Visual markers: Icons
Where different language backgrounds exist, visual symbols or icons are used to facilitate the communication of information between them. With the rapid spread of Internet applications, the use of visual symbolic imagery has increased – the World Wide Web gives access to an enormous variety of content to people all over the world from hugely diverse cultural, national and language backgrounds. Using visually symbolic imagery appears to make sense for several reasons: Quite apart from language barriers, script can be difficult to read on the screen, especially when it has to be small in order to fit the size of a button. What little space is available in the design of a button can be filled more memorably with characteristic imagery and colours. The use of icons is a viable alternative in a medium that is less suitable for printed verbal representation. Good icon design reduces messages to their bare essentials and avoids unnecessary detail which might appear blurred and ugly in pixels. However, national sensibilities about colour for instance have to be taken into consideration for the design. A successful icon conveys an idea clearly, it is abstract, easily recognisable and executed in a formally attractive way.

In order to judge an icon, the previously mentioned parameters can be reviewed empirically. A further possibility lies in an analysis at the semiotic parameter such as the syntactic, semantic and pragmatic. Here the designer should not forget to also review the bond between icon and user interface: The functions and navigations are often controlled through the icon.

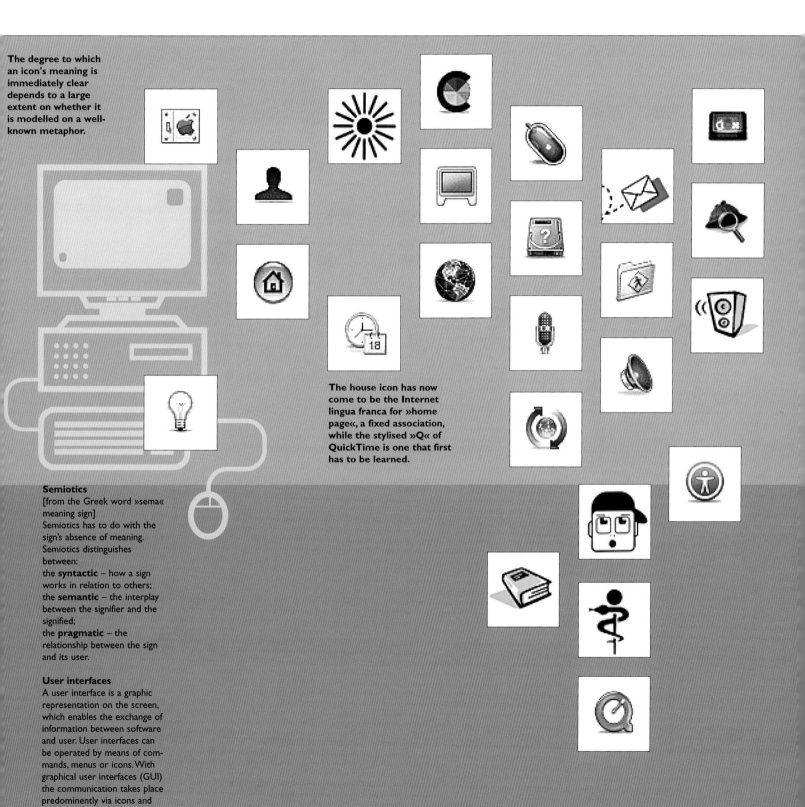

Good icons are abstract and easily recognisable, they are stylistically formal and relay a clear idea.

The degree to which an icon's meaning is immediately clear depends to a large extent on whether it is modelled on a well-known metaphor.

The house icon has now come to be the Internet lingua franca for »home page«, a fixed association, while the stylised »Q« of QuickTime is one that first has to be learned.

Semiotics
[from the Greek word »sema« meaning sign]
Semiotics has to do with the sign's absence of meaning. Semiotics distinguishes between:
the **syntactic** – how a sign works in relation to others;
the **semantic** – the interplay between the signifier and the signified;
the **pragmatic** – the relationship between the sign and its user.

User interfaces
A user interface is a graphic representation on the screen, which enables the exchange of information between software and user. User interfaces can be operated by means of commands, menus or icons. With graphical user interfaces (GUI) the communication takes place predominently via icons and windows.

3.04

088.**089**

Alternatives:
Symbols and icons

Overriding criteria for designing a good icon should be clarity, comprehensibility and content. Constraints of image resolution and the pixel grid make a minimalist design avoiding unnecessary detail more suitable.

»Original thought comes in images.«
Arthur Schopenhauer

Step-by-step abstraction of an icon for the service sector:
The original idea stems from the depiction of tools in the real world: screwdriver, pincers, hammer.

For screen depiction the tools have too much detail. Leaving out colours gives clearer emphasis to the shape.

Concentrating on the characteristic detail of a tool, which is subsequently adapted to poor screen resolution by enlargement and further abstraction. Avoid curves and diagonals.

2.1

The icons below change mood, and hence significance, depending on the use of colour.

With blue the icon suggests something sterile and clean.

With blood-red, cynicism overrides the meaning of this icon. With orange it could be in a Flyer for »Dance Till You Drop«.

1.1

Inventing an icon

When devising an icon, clarity, easy recognition, and abstraction are of overriding importance, as is the considered application of colour. Colour can fundamentally change the basic stance of an icon, whether it appears neutral and functional in cool blue, or emotional and energetic in red (1.1). When choosing a colour, specifics of perception in other cultures must be considered at all times (see pages 38, 39). This also applies to plants and animals (1.2).
Another criterion to be considered is the pixel grid. Often, no more than 30 to 50 pixel^2 is available for an icon. Being aware of these constraints combined with restrictions in image resolution make it easy to understand how appropriate design compromises must be made. Avoid diagonal lines and curves, and omit detail. Good results can be achieved through the reduction of detail and application of a zoom-effect (2.1). In the absence, as yet, of a universally suitable verbal or visual language for the medium it is best to base designs on clichéd analogies from the non-virtual world to ensure the correct execution of instructions. Hence, an icon with an arrow and an envelope is immediately understood (see page 86).
Symbols such as a briefcase in which to deposit your data or a dustbin for erasing them are equally successful.

Computer-to-film
Computertomogram
Comhograp

1.2

With the universal reach of the Internet the designer must be aware of cultural sensibilities when using specific colours or objects. Hence the owl in the West stands for wisdom, whilst signifying Black Magic and sorcery in Central America (and in Harry Potter). The owl as a symbol for wisdom in the Western World: Above, icons from a digital encyclopaedia **(blue owls) and an icon (yellow owl) used by the publishers Palace Athene.**

Universally accepted icons should not be given a new context. A new icon should be designed for every new operation. As a symbol for unpleasant smells the dustbin icon is incomprehensible.

In the absence of a specific language for the Internet it is best for the designer to maintain the use of standard accepted analogies.

Icons using standard elements, and hence a uniform aesthetic, are easiest for the user to understand.

    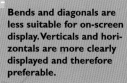

For the essential minimalist effect of an icon, selecting one characteristic detail is often sufficient.

Bends and diagonals are less suitable for on-screen display. Verticals and horizontals are more clearly displayed and therefore preferable.

Alternative studies for pictograms by the agency Mutabor.

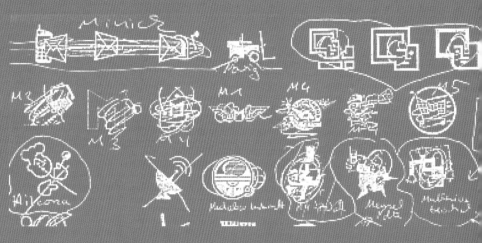

Pictogram sketches by the agency Mutabor.

3.04

Alternatives:
Digital assistants

The range of possibilities afforded by new media is still not fully applied. Try voice or visual animation instead of poorly displayed text.

»We should be aware that machines
will take over one day.«
Alan Turing

Any visitor to the **NASA** website will be met by a virtual assistant giving useful hints and making casual cheeky remarks, following you around and standing by your side like a good companion.
A virtual assistant does not need to simulate the human form in order to relate to the user.

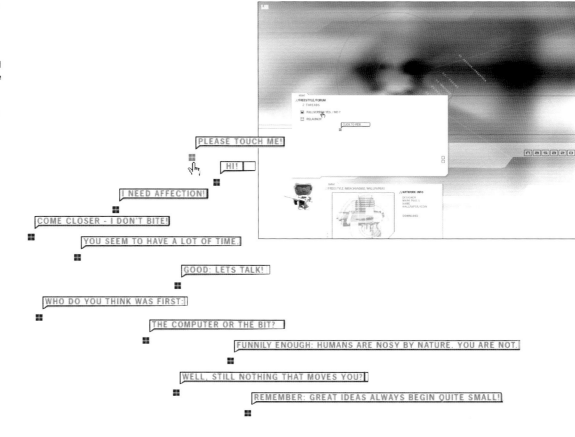

PLEASE TOUCH ME!

HI!

I NEED AFFECTION!

COME CLOSER - I DON'T BITE!

YOU SEEM TO HAVE A LOT OF TIME.

GOOD: LETS TALK!

WHO DO YOU THINK WAS FIRST:

THE COMPUTER OR THE BIT?

FUNNILY ENOUGH: HUMANS ARE NOSY BY NATURE. YOU ARE NOT.

WELL, STILL NOTHING THAT MOVES YOU?

REMEMBER: GREAT IDEAS ALWAYS BEGIN QUITE SMALL!

Digital assistants

Given the opportunities for action and animation, new media are infinitely more flexible than paper.
A range of interactive assistants, guides, and showmasters are available to enhance visual communication as an alternative to verbal communication in an international context. These assistants can only be as intelligent as their creators.
When devising the animation and its usefulness, keep a clearly defined target group and its needs in mind: you would probably not sell a pension scheme through animated comics.

It may be advisable to have an assistant appear and enter into dialogue with the user by request only.

These virtual figures may perform various roles: when taking you through a site, they may be there continuously to point out and explain features in the manner of a tourist guide. Alternatively, the assistant may be less prominent and appear only by request, communicating with the user and answering his or her questions only when help is needed.

When designing an animated **Info Clip**, remember that any verbal content cannot be printed. Including a print link might be helpful.

talk to me

Atira

Guten Tag! Ich heiße Atira und begleite Sie durch die Website von shopping24. Verraten Sie mir bitte Ihren Namen?

Ihr Name ▸ Veruschka

absenden

On the Shopping 24 website the user will be welcomed by a personal best friend and taken on a shopping tour. Atira, the digital assistant, will not just provide useful hints for presents but can help with more general queries, such as what the time is.

Similarly FinBot will answer questions about finances after having asked the visitor for his or her name.

Nett Sie zu treffen, Veruschka. Am liebsten berichte ich natürlich über unsere Shops oder über meinen Arbeitgeber shopping24. Was möchten Sie wissen?

Wie spät ist es?

Meine innere Uhr sagt, es ist jetzt 16:13:02.

Wo gibt es tolle Geschenke?

Für diesen Anlass finden Sie bestimmt bei Hawesko einen edlen Wein oder eine leckere Delikatesse. Oder schauen Sie bei dem Otto Supermarkt Service herein. Auch Blumen sind immer wieder ein schönes Geschenk. Dazu bietet Valentins oder Blume2000 alles, was das Herz begehrt.

Eliza
(by Jo Weizenbaum, 1966)
Eliza is a computer program where the user can communicate with a virtual therapist. The program will react to text input. Eliza is programmed to form new sentences from a sensible selection of catch-phrases and thus simulate real understanding. This nearly forty year old experiment in artificial intelligence has not provided the answer to the challenge of real understanding.

```
User:  Men are all alike.
ELIZA: In what way?
User:  They're always bugging us
       about something or other.
ELIZA: Can you think of a specific
       example?
User:  Well, my boyfriend made me
       come here.
ELIZA: Your boyfriend made you come
       here?
User:  He says I'm depressed much
       of the time.
ELIZA: I am sorry to hear that you
       are depressed.
User:  It's true. I am unhappy.
ELIZA: Do you think coming here will
       help you not to be unhappy?
User:  I need some help, that much
       seems certain.
ELIZA: What would it mean to you if
       you got some help?
User:  Perhaps I could learn to get
       along with my mother.
ELIZA: Tell me more about your
       family.

(...)
```

3.04

092.**093**

Alternatives:
Showmasters and
emoticons

The presence of new media and modern
technology is vivid and their success depends
on the visual communication of information.

»I often think there should exist
a special typographical sign for a smile –
some sort of concave mark, a supine round bracket,
which I would now like to trace in reply to your question.«
Vladimir Nabokov

Instead of written text,
the merits of a flea-potion
manufactured by **Bayer**
are advertised by a dog
in a quiz show.

The Internet user will
immediately empathise
with his own beloved pet.
The sales drive is commu-
nicated via an element of
humour to hit straight at
the heart of any dog lover.
Success is achieved without
resorting to conventional
scientific advice on some
non-descript medical site.

Bring those
here and let me host your
website, handsome.

Is the Internet about
to turn into a medium
of gestures?
In other industries that
are dealing with inter-
national clients communi-
cation is already based on
gestures: think of the way
flight attendants explain
emergency procedures
to airline passengers.

Showmaster Showmasters are an extension of the concept
of the animated assistant taking visitors through
a website. Similarly to television and film the
Internet makes use of multimedia applications
such as sound and animated images. Once speed
for data transmission on the Internet has
improved, the use of such applications will become
more common.

A speaker called **Larry**
gives a talk on one of
the most frequently
used words in the English
language: the F-word.
The observer becomes
a listener. Brief illustrations

appear. The visual anima-
tion of the mouth is extremely rudimentary, yet
effective.

F WORD

strike (strk)
v. struck (strk), struck or
strick·en (strkn), strik·ing,
strikes.

1. To hit sharply, as with the
hand, the fist, or a weapon.

Fucking beautiful

All the FUCKING WORK

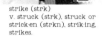

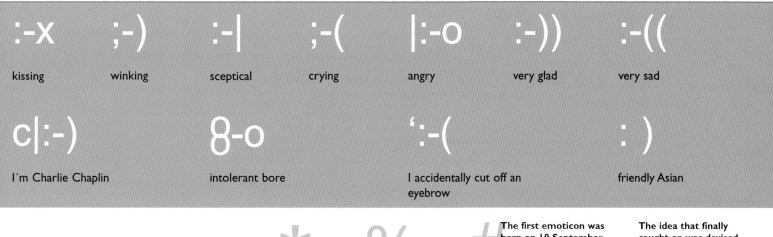

:-X	;-)	:-|	;-(	|:-o	:-))	:-((
kissing	winking	sceptical	crying	angry	very glad	very sad

c|:-)	8-o	':-(	:)
I'm Charlie Chaplin	intolerant bore	I accidentally cut off an eyebrow	friendly Asian

The first emoticons, 1982.

The first emoticon was born on 19 September 1982. Some practical joker had put a hoax alarm on the university public notice board, whereupon all lifts were put out of order. In the aftermath it was considered how to mark such jocular warnings in future. Suggestions such as * or % marks were the »smiley's« first predecessors. The # sign held its own for a while, marking the joker's bared teeth.

The idea that finally caught on was devised by information scientist Scott Fahlman. His was the first horizontal type. It was the »smiley« which became universally popular and has since been used in thousands of variations: in now countless e-mails there are smiles, winks, and curses.

Emoticons

Emoticons or smileys are faces made up from font signs. They are widely used in Internet applications where there is little scope for visual expression, such as e-mails. A fun-loving group of users apply them to express emotion in order to save time with unnecessary words. They are used for the same purpose in SMS messages, expressing emotion on the other end with maximum typing economy. What began with a misunderstanding more than 20 years ago has snowballed into a universal system of communication to overcome any language restrictions. Building on a basic and universally accepted vocabulary it leaves enough room for individual creativity.

19-Sep-82 11:44 Scott E Fahlman
From: Scott E <Fahlman at CMU-20C>

I propose that the following
character sequence for joke markers:
:-)

Read it sideways. Actually, it is
probably more economical to mark
things that are NOT jokes, given
current trends. For this, use
:-(

Eroticons:

Woman: slim...

...voluptuous variety

Man

4

techniques: **how to use type in grids**

095

How should typography be incorporated in a screen grid?
What is the best way of using typography in the restricted space of a mini display?

4.01

E-learning sites
Information sites

In websites and CD-Roms, which mainly communicate factual information, text must be easy to absorb for the reader.

»I think anything we take in with our eyes should be poured out over all the shapes we can see.
Consider, too, the letters, the punctuation marks, which order our thoughts.«
El Lissitzky

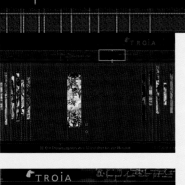

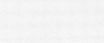

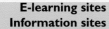

The colours in the Trojan website (shades of grey and green, and black) convey calm and respectability. The colours were chosen for their muted brightness which doesn't clash with the text, and enhances readability.
Orange, with its energetic quality, is reserved solely for text or other elements to aid navigation or orientation. Yet, in spite of the selective use of orange, its vitality permeates the entire presentation without obstructing readability.

E-learning sites
Information sites

Considering respective emphasis of specific design parameters such as typography, colour, use of images, distribution of elements (layout), overall mood, navigation and orientation will depend on the target group and overall content of the on-screen presentation. Before starting to work, any designer should ensure he knows his target group and the content of the presentation.

A well-designed page of information or e-learning with a clear layout will facilitate the reader's ability to concentrate on factual content. Avoid confounding the visitor by unfavourably designed text and difficult orientation, when he or she is already faced with a challenging learning programme or complicated factual content.

E-learning sites
Information sites
: factual information must be
 easy-to-grasp.
Type
– recommended minimum
 size 12 pt.
– select font for good readability on screen, avoid serifs.
– no more than an average 7 to
 8 words per line.
– distinctive colour contrast
 to set off font from the
 background but avoid glaring
 clashes.

e principal colours
this science site are
ey and blue, conveying
ectivity and intellect.

The grey font on a white
background is easy to read,
without clashing too
strongly, which would
have happened with
black text.

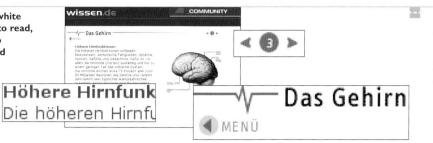

When designing informa-
tion on screen, ease of
navigation and orientation
are just as important as
the choice of easy-to-read
fonts.

Das Troia-Projekt.

A linear structure is common in learning or factual
websites: neither the font
nor a complicated structure should irritate the visitor. A linear approach to
guide the visitor through
the factual content is an
obvious choice. It is im-
portant though, to let the
user choose to return to
the starter page, whenever
he or she wishes.

The content in the Trojan
site on the left is arranged
in a linear succession of
short bits of information,
distinguished by their
colour. You navigate with
a jump-to-top button at
the end of each box.

: **Beigaben aus Grab 21** des Friedhofs
in der Besik-Bucht, dem Hafen von
Troia (um 1300 v. Chr.).
Das mykenische Gefäß, eventuell

| 10 | 20 | 30 | 36 |

Short columns with a
maximum of eight words
to the line enhance
readability on screen.
Particularly with the right
choice of font and size
(Verdana 12 pt), and
colour contrast seen here.
Glare-free black for the
background combined with
a cream font is a good choice for excellent readability.
The combination is much
more favourable than the
hard contrast of white.

4.0I

Reference material
Information sites

It is essential that the required information within the content can be found quickly and is easy to take in. Typography should be applied with all available parameters of emphasis.

»PINGUE PECUS DOMINO FACIAS ET CETERA PRAETER INGENIUM.«
(Let my cattle and other things be fat, but not my mind.)
Horaz

A clear and concise layout using simple typographical means.
Varieties of emphasis:
Enlarging font size (header/subject)
Colour highlighting font (header/text)
or when activating a topic –
whilst other menu points remain transparent.

Stock-Exchange
Die Welt des Börsenparketts.
heute ein riskanter Volksspo

Headline | subject
Navigation | subject

Subject | explanation

Navigation | general

Reference material should be designed to look topical and uncluttered.

Colour as used to emphasise the topicality of the subject matter presented in a dictionary of the **New Economy**:
The combination of shades of green, blue, and turquoise with white and contrasted with some black creates a fresh mood.
Seemingly transparent planes intensify the impression.

The overall design is well structured and follows a horizontal layout.
The website avoids typographical clutter: there is only one font type, though applied with variety in size and emphasis. Headings or topical items are emphasised by enlarged font sizes or differentiated in colour.

Reference material
Information sites

With reference material or topical items the user needs to be able to get an overall view quickly and easily. Information should be concise and easily found. Hence the designer should use simple means to set up intelligible hierarchical structures. Any design which is too complex will affect time taken to gather information and the overall impression of the site as concise, up to date, and reliable suffers too.

Reference sites
Information sites
: easy-to-gather information.
Type
– use font emphasis – such as typeface, colour, size – to arrange information hierarchically.

Various applications of type emphasis are suitable to facilitate quick intake and identification of respective levels of hierarchy in online news magazines and newspapers.

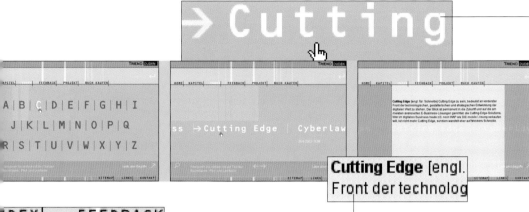

Hierarchical arrangement by means of simple typographical tools.
Emphasis:
Bigger font size (subject) and colour (activation)

Differentiation by means of simple typographical tools.
Emphasis:
Differentiating between bold and normal typefaces helps to distinguish search terms from other background information.

Differentiation by means of simple typographical tools.
Emphasis:
Using Versalia (upper case letters) for menu headings distinguishes them from other fonts and makes them easy to identify for navigation. Font size with easy-to-read Versalia can be kept small in navigation as only short words are necessary here.

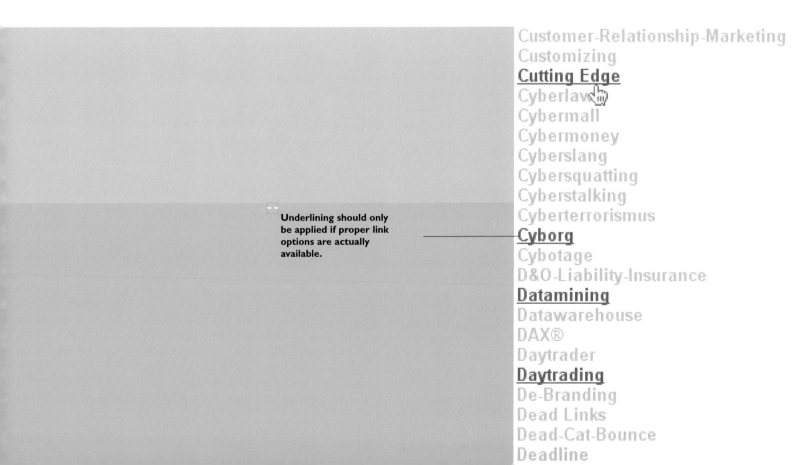

Underlining should only be applied if proper link options are actually available.

4.01

Search engines

You do not want to waste time looking to find something. Hence search engines should have a tightly ordered structure. Typography, colour, and structure have to be functional and avoid distraction.

»I've always been a friend of order, and want to read my regular weekly paper until my dying days«
Johann Wolfgang von Goethe

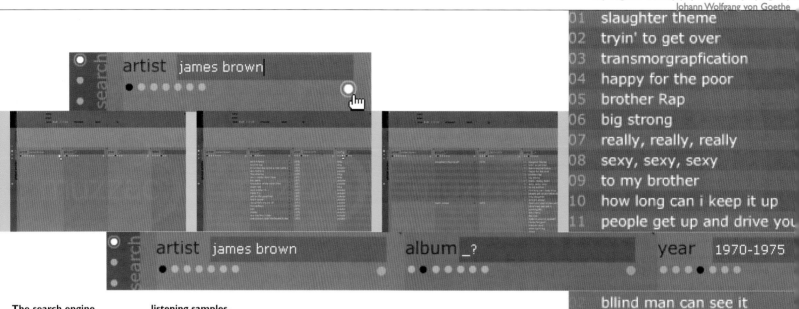

01	slaughter theme
02	tryin' to get over
03	transmorgrapfication
04	happy for the poor
05	brother Rap
06	big strong
07	really, really, really
08	sexy, sexy, sexy
09	to my brother
10	how long can i keep it up
11	people get up and drive you

bllind man can see it
sporting life
dirty harry
the boss
make it good to yourself
mama feelgood
mama's daed
white lightning
chase

The search engine »Muzzac« provides an interactive archive of music catering for the industry. It offers a high standard of user comfort and a logical structure to master a huge variety of search criteria and content arranged through text, lyrics, graphics, video, and

listening samples. The design is reduced to the bare essentials in order to give maximum scope to order music and the associated complex content.

Search engines
You do not want to waste time looking for something. Any designer of search engines should create logical hierarchies for ease of orientation. The subject bar must be given overall prominence and stand out from any other information. The same applies for the search button to start the machine. The engine usually offers further options once information has been found. It should follow a well thought-out pattern to further structure content and prevent the user from being swamped in text.

Both subject bar and search button are clearly distinguishable in their three-dimensional design

Search engines
: speedy location of information.
Type
– recommended minimum size 12 pt.
– good screen readability, avoid serifs.
– structure content through emphasis (colour, typeface, underlay of coloured background) and introduction of logical hierarchies with different font sizes.

Hierarchical order through variations in colour and tonality, font size, and typeface.

Too much variety in the application of emphasis can be confusing. Restricting emphasis to where it is relevant is preferable.

Verdana 16 pt
for headers and song titles.
Verdana 12 pt
for all other levels of information content.

song: think
artist: james brown
time: 3:12 / -2:53   released: 1973   label: polidor   lp: the payback
lyrics tabs contribution biografie interviews relations visual

Heeeeeyow
Think about the sacrifi
Think about the good t
Now think of all the ba

More leading (space between lines) in favour of better readability.

Structuring and ordering design elements are minimalistic: a white font contrasted with a grey or black background denotes search terminology, headers, or successful hits. Verdana was used throughout, in three different sizes:
Verdana 16 pt
for headers and song titles,
Verdana 14 pt
for text and other content,
Verdana 12 pt
for all other levels of information content.

Leading was increased by 2 pt per size to improve readability and ease of intake of textual content.

If grey seems somewhat dull, the background colour may be adjusted, whilst maintaining font colour.

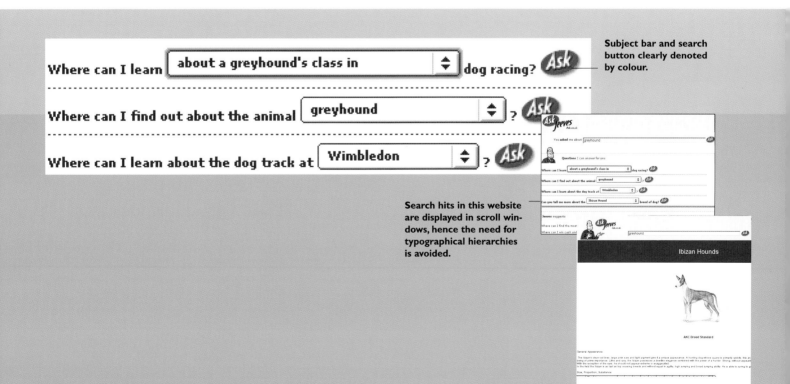

Where can I learn | about a greyhound's class in ⇕ | dog racing? Ask

Where can I find out about the animal | greyhound ⇕ | ? Ask Jeeves

Where can I learn about the dog track at | Wimbledon ⇕ | ? Ask

Subject bar and search button clearly denoted by colour.

Search hits in this website are displayed in scroll windows, hence the need for typographical hierarchies is avoided.

4.0I

Image sites |
products (fashion)

Image sites (fashion and luxury goods) are designed
primarily as conveyors of atmosphere: everything
towards this aim is permitted.

»Seeing is believing – the appearance is the reality
German saying

Image sites
Fashion and luxury goods

Image sites advertising lifestyle products, especially
fashion or luxury goods, are often more
concerned with presenting the mood of a brand
philosophy rather than with presenting a full range
of goods or exhaustive product information.
Expressing the full extent of the required mood
presents a real challenge to the designer.
Expressing mood, through colour, atmosphere,
type, layout, and animation, supersedes any
readability of information. One aim is to captivate
new target groups – the design should appeal
to their sense of belonging and identification.
Alternatively, the design's appeal should consolida-
te the loyalty of existing target groups.

**Different to the timeless
sense of the Van Laack site,
the Fornarina site presents
itself in a fast-living and
trashy light. Fashion fades
quickly, and the visitor's
impression of this site is
being at the heart of
trendiness. Here, the font is
used as an analogy to the
latest catwalk trends with
its prominent shading,
glaring colours, and
complementary contrasts.**

Image sites |
Fashion and luxury goods
: convey mood.
Type
– semantic application of type
and colour as an appropriate
expression of brand philosophy and associated
atmosphere.

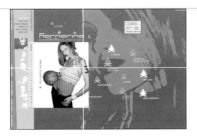

Various items can be given priority by the screen designer through their position on screen: elements in the upper left of the screen tend to get noticed first, those positioned in the lower right are noticed last, unless rising to prominence in animations or pop-ups.

Van Laack shirts tend to be worn for business rather than for their cult value: the uncluttered look of Van Laack gives an impression of clarity, timelessness and elegance for the brand and hence for its products with which the visitor can identify. Fonts are used with tasteful restraint.

They are either overlaid transparently on the images or well integrated with the background colours.

Mit Hemden ist es wie mit Ul
genügend Erfahrung gesammelt,
bedeutet dabei, nicht nur den A
eigenen zu genügen. Darum gil
zur Schau gestellter Luxus – son
eigenen Wohlgefühls.

‹‹

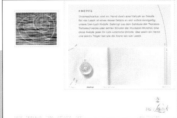

Signet
Stoffe
Kragen
Knöpfe
Manschetten
Taschen

Kings   Atelier   Kollektic

FASHION   ▶ INSIDE WORMLAND

The brand Wormland's credo is proclaimed as fashion with style and a range to fit uncompromising customer satisfaction. Accordingly, the website presentation is suitably non-controversial: warm colours, well co-ordinated, without provocation. The font is unspectacular, easy to read, and well integrated with the colour sense and general structure.

Im Privatleben widmete sich Theo Wormland leidenschaftlich der Kunst. Seine bedeutende Sammlung von Gemälden und Skulpturen

4.01

Image sites | services

An image site (service) should provide a brief introduction to a business and the services it offers, arouse the visitor's curiosity, as well as leaving an impression of reliability and trustworthiness.

»You never know what is enough
unless you know what is more than enough.«
William Blake

THIS SITE IS MAKES
INTENSIUE USE OF MEDIA:

ISDN OR BETTER_RECOMMENDED
56K _ON YOUR OWN RISK
BELOW_FORGET IT_SORRY

REQUIREMENTS:
BROWSER 5.X _ FLASH 5 _ QT 4

Semantic application of a font:
A desired impression can be created by the sheer visual impact of the selected font.

The e-zine »industrial culture« uses a contrived font to prepare the visitor for the subject of bionic man, the robot.

On image sites text should be easy to assimilate.
This is successfully achieved in the Chromagan website:
The reader is introduced to the subject painlessly by the hierarchical structure of the text.
The white font features prominently and is easy to read on the reduced brightness of the coloured background.
Furthermore, a good size

was chosen for the font and length of lines.

Header — Denoting subject matter.

Teaser — Introduces the subject, engages the reader's interest.

Text — Explains the subject.

Faszination Roboter

Roboter begegnen uns als riesige Metall-monster, menschenähnliche Androiden und winzige Hightech-Wunder.

Sie bewegen sich auf Rädern, Rollen oder Ketten, auf Schrauben, Beinen oder Wurmgliedern fort; sie schweben im Weltraum oder krabbeln am Meeresboden,

10	20	30	40

Image sites
Services

Businesses use image sites to provide a concise and intelligible introduction to the nature of their goods and services. Similarly to the image sites of fashion and luxury goods industries the attention lies with creating an atmosphere through the use of type, colour, and layout. Simultaneously the visitor's curiosity about the business should be aroused and his or her trust in what is on offer raised. However, contrary to the fashion sites, content is conveyed through text and not through visuals and ephemeral impressions. Any net visitor is impatient: Textual content should be kept short and more casual than in formal print to enhance accessibility. The reader wants concise and easy to assimilate information, best introduced by a little teaser of no more than a couple of lines. The teaser provides the reader with basic information and may subsequently encourage him to pursue the subject further. Text should not be too long, instead it should be clearly structured by short sentences, avoiding the need to scroll.

Image sites | Services
: text easy to assimilate.
Type
– recommended minimum size 12 pt.
– good screen readability, avoid serifs.
– hierarchically structured layout.
– easy reading of line content of no more than 5 to 10 words.

**Design agencies:
one industry, different
messages.**

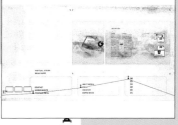

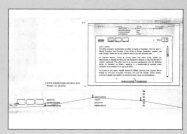

Lauri J. Slavill
The most successful partnerships are often synergies of opposites. Attorney Lauri J. Slavill, Executive Vice President of the Winds of Change Foundation, provides just such strategic ballast for the foundation's visionary founder Shameya Gilo.

The agency »Sadee«
presents itself with a clear
concept and careful detail.
Font size bordering on
what can still be distinguished on screen and long
lines of text are never-
theless pleasant to read.
The reason lies with an

otherwise logical and
uncluttered surface design
which does not distract
the user when he or she is
reading.

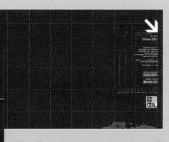

The French agency »3e
Oeil« offers a complex
service which is matched
by a complex presentation
design.

The font is, however,
remarkably simple:
pleasantly sized, white,
distinguishable from the
background, with good
line lengths.

bout us

utting it simply, you could say we provide
ervices for Branding, Interactive and
rint design. We just say we like design.
o, we *love* design. We *love* how it makes

The website for »formul8«
follows the motto »less is
more« with its austere use
of only one colour, red, in
a range of tonalities.
The basic tone is set by
red, the various elements
are distinguished only by
their varying tonalities with
text being the lightest and
as a result appearing as the
core of the page.

4.01

Shopping sites

Shopping sites should seduce and entice you into making a purchase: information should be conveyed quickly, navigation should be simple and supported by an uncluttered design structure.

»Advertising is a friendly sod.«
Oliviero Toscani

A very easy to read, compact grotesque font is used for the book reviews. The effect is enhanced by narrow columns, an appropriate sized font, and good col contrast setting off light type against the darker background.

The Phaidon Press website is presented on darkly coloured pages.
The prominence of the reviews and books for sale is clearly denoted by their light colours. The way to the shopping basket is outlined in a light coloured font.

Shopping sites
: create a good overall impression and enticement to buy.
Type
– recommended minimum size 12 pt.
– good screen readability, avoid serifs.
– unified typographical concept (restricted use of one font with variety of emphasis e.g. Arial, Arial bold etc.) for unified and logical overall impression.
– colour distinction for words leading to the »basket«.

Shopping sites On shopping sites the user may purchase goods and services, or just obtain the required product information. Usually impatient, the user expects to reach his or her goal quickly. The task of the designer is to subtly and persuasively entice both those initially seeking information only, as well as hesitant visitors to come to a decision to purchase. Any potential consumer buys not merely the product, but also the way the product is presented.

Any more blatant use of colour and font is likely to raise the visitor's suspicions about the value-for-money of the product on offer, especially in a medium significantly lacking a haptic, tactile dimension. A comparatively easy remedy may be an appropriately relevant product description, the effectiveness of which is enhanced by short lines which can be read at a glance, a good sized font, as well as sufficient background contrast. If the information is absorbed successfully, the way to the shopping basket should be clearly laid out for both hesitant and determined shoppers to facilitate a speedy purchase. This could, for instance, be achieved by emphasising font by colour, which is either selected specifically or derived from the colours of the brand logo.

Beluga Caviar, 7 oz. (Russia) *

In the current tight caviar market, securing the best requires the best connections. Our supplier hand-picks his stock from the top Caspan Sea sources and delivers a consistently exceptional product—no small feat. From the largest sturgeon, the largest and most precious of the pearls because they take twenty years to mature. Steel grey and buttery rich, they taste

CAVIAR

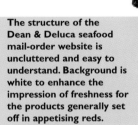

The structure of the Dean & Deluca seafood mail-order website is uncluttered and easy to understand. Background is white to enhance the impression of freshness for the products generally set off in appetising reds.

Product information can be read at a glance, benefiting from brevity and simple font typographical design.

Logical navigation: simple typographical design, grotesque font, black on white.

Baking
Beans, Nuts & Seeds
Butcher Shop
> **Caviar**
 •Caviar Service
 •Sturgeon Caviar
Charcuterie & Foie Gras
Cheese
Chocolates & Confections
Coffee & Cocoa

to [(Billing) ‡] Qty [1] **Order**

item comes directly from our supplier, and may
uire up to 48 hours to ship.

his item requires Next Day Shipping.

O head board
● head box

[⊞⊞⊞] [look] [edit] [+] [−] [↺]

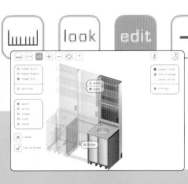

There is hardly any text on the »Kitchen« website where the user can assemble his or her own kitchen from a variety of modules on offer: it operates with the visitor's sense of fun and creative curiosity.

SEARCH THE STORE !
◉ ALL
○ ARTIST NAME
○ RELEASE TITLE
○ TRACK NAME

Navigation and emphasis of type are defined through colour of the logo.

ARTIST:	JEANS TEAM	PRICE:	
TITLE:	gold und silber CDM	7.5 €	
RELEASE:	09/27/02	CDM	
RATING:	○ ○ ○ ○ ○		BUY !

Community sites

Community sites require a subtle design to appeal
to the sense of identification of a select target group.

»Across every border, [...] village, and town,
proletarians of all nations, unite!«
Leo Trotsky

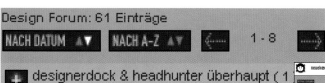

Design Forum: 61 Einträge

NACH DATUM ▲▼   NACH A-Z ▲▼   ⟨....   1 - 8   ....⟩

➕ designerdock & headhunter überhaupt (1

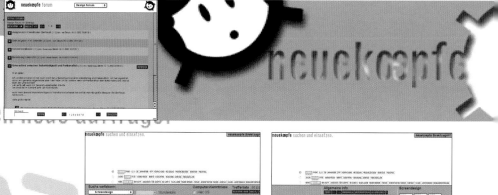

The »neuekoepfe-forum«
is a community to match
designers with potential
clients. Both client and
designer can present
themselves individually.
They can be searched by
category, information and
press can be exchanged.

The seriousness of the
undertaking is echoed in
the design: there is a solid
blue background, with text
in a blue grotesque font
appears restrained and is
easy to read. Red type is
used for emphasis. The site
avoids gratuitous effects,
which makes it a successful
forum forum reliability and
qualified exchange.

Screendesign

Deutschland ⬍ Land

Community sites   These are sites for the qualified exchange of
opinion and information, or forums for an
entertaining chat with other members. With
community sites their subject grouping as well
as the design has to transmit to the visitor who
the other members are and what their motives
might be. The visitor to forums of serious
exchange expects a reliable treatment of subject
matter and of the privacy of his or her own
identity, something that is often neglected on the
Internet. A subtle selection of type and colour can
achieve the desired effect of reliability.

Community sites
Forums for business and
specialised subjects
: detailed exchange of
information
Type
– recommended minimum size
  12 pt.
– font selected for good
  readability on screen,
  avoid serifs.
– unified appearance of type
  (use of only one font, with
  variations in emphasis e.g.
  Arial, Arial bold, etc.).
– reduced brightness either
  for font or background,
  avoid glaring colours.

You must each find your instrument, and meet back at the gold discs. Good luck!

gregmoore1: do u know the way ??

gregmoore1: ringo take key

~Cin~: dudler is from berlin

EmilyEvil: do you have aol instant messanger?

canislunaris: I have a piece of the Wall hanging in my atelier in a plastic bag

The »helpgames« community meets to chat in a bar-cum-lounge, or in a games room to look for the instruments played by the Beatles. When all the instruments have been found, the Beatles start performing. This community meets for entertainment, and the design is treated accordingly: Shaded and bold fonts, occasionally totally unreadable, are placed on various coloured backgrounds. The unconventional design is justified by the emphasis on speed, lightheartedness and fun, rather than serious content.

Community sites
Entertainment
: leisure and amusement.
Type
– recommended minimum size 12 pt.
– experimental treatment of font to underline expression and mood rather than readability. Use »trendy« fonts, dynamic colour contrasts between font and background for exuberance and inviting appeal, and to enhance the sense of fun and games (warm colours).

4.01

Games sites

110.111

A lot of time is spent on games sites, but not for legibility: consequently text may be treated for instant recognition and easy consumption, or itself acquire a playful dimension, flashy and over the top.

»I won, and twenty minutes later I left the gaming room with hundred and seventy guilders in my pocket. [...]
That's what your last guilder can do!
What if I'd lost courage, not taken the decision?
Tomorrow, tomorrow, it'll all be over!«
Feodor Dostoevsky

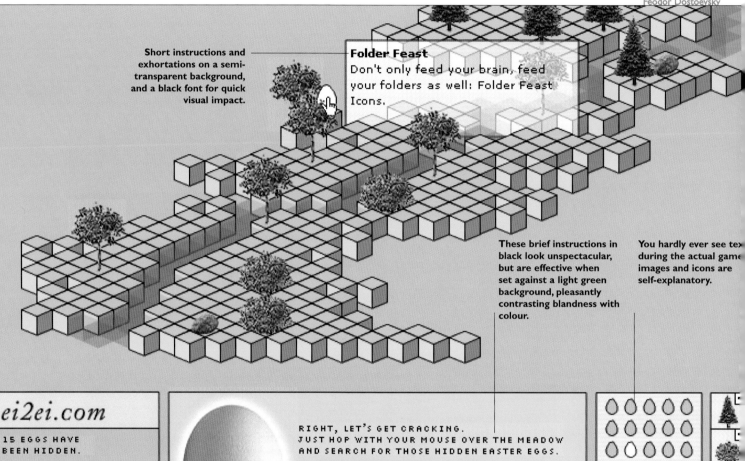

Short instructions and exhortations on a semi-transparent background, and a black font for quick visual impact.

Folder Feast
Don't only feed your brain, feed your folders as well: Folder Feast Icons.

These brief instructions in black look unspectacular, but are effective when set against a light green background, pleasantly contrasting blandness with colour.

You hardly ever see tex during the actual game images and icons are self-explanatory.

ei2ei.com

15 EGGS HAVE BEEN HIDDEN.

RIGHT, LET'S GET CRACKING.
JUST HOP WITH YOUR MOUSE OVER THE MEADOW
AND SEARCH FOR THOSE HIDDEN EASTER EGGS.

Games sites The disposition of many an Internet user to spend time playing games is matched by a dislike for even the slightest distraction by text: he or she wants to start playing immediately! The game should open straight away. Instructions should come via sample demonstrations without text, or with very brief explanations in the margin. With tediously long instructions, the surfer will leave the site as soon as he or she has accessed it. Hence the text design should ensure that instructions are presented in small, easily digestible sections. Telegram-style instructions can either undergo conventional typographical design treatment (typeface, font size, length of line, colour contrast) or be treated as playful eye-catchers. Given the appropriate brevity of text as outlined, the application of strong colour contrast, blown-up or distorted shaded fonts may be just as effective.

A pause option to interrupt play is the only really essential function in a game. Typographically it must be instantaneously distinctive in order to prevent an obsessive player from being caught out by a ringing telephone or sneaky boss.

Games sites
: quick assimilation of text (e.g. rules of the game).
Type
– short text, short lines.
– recommended minimum size 12 pt.
– good screen readability, avoid serifs.
– selected words as eye-catchers through size, font raised from the background by colour, or use of unusual typeface.
– animated type.

Egg-Pile
All players take a seat around the table. Pile up some salt in the middle of the table. An Easter egg goes on top. Each

Egg-
All pl
and
troug
to ea

Linux
salmon, lace of champagne, frozen spinach, cream, black and white pepper, salt

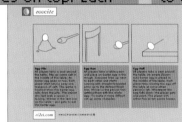

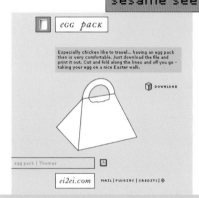

Sleeping Tiger
scallions, shitake-mushrooms, bell pepper, ginger, garlic, peppers, soy souce, sugar, sesame seeds

e non-game pages of 2ei.com (Ei is German egg) are an amusing eatment of anything ated to eggs: you can lect your favourite ocolate Easter Bunny a »Bunny Contest«, see the best games to played with an egg der »Eggcite«, get a cipe under »Eggsquisite«, see the demonstration an »Egg pack«.

The textual sections are easy to read for their brevity, good choice of font size combined with appropriately sized columns and good colour contrast between font and background. Furthermore, text sections are competently partitio-ned. This caters well to a target group that is young and fun-loving, and obvious-ly does not want to be lectured on the subject.

Many games, such as the recent »black&white2« by Peter Molyneux, are based solely on images and animation, and manage to do entirely without text.

4.01

Beyond tasteful design

112.113

Certain enterprises on the net intentionally go beyond the limits of good taste. Where the emphasis is on speed and good value, type is used as a blatant advertising tool.

»Sex sells.«
Advertising wisdom

Big on gesture: the expressionistic qualities advertising the merits of erotic content sites lay not only in the exaggerated facial expressions of the protagonists, but also in the application of blatant typography that contravenes all rules of good design. Such exhibitionistic design can only be achieved if you have no sense of design propriety at all, or a knowledge thorough enough to allow you to intentionally break all the golden rules of good design.

Beyond good design

Internet businesses such as erotic content sites or cut-price value sales sites intentionally ignore the merits of typography for its readability in favour of an illustrative gesture to carry blatant and condensed information. Things appear exclusive and for »free«, as long as you progress quickly enough to miss the small print. With this in mind type is applied with all the emphasis necessary to ensure its outstanding prominence.

Erotic sites
: significant gestures to boost sexual excitement and emotion.
Type
– font treated semantically: any impact-boosting parameters may be applied; glaring colours, shaded fonts, perpendicular words, blown-up font sizes, etc.
– italics to underline impression of volatility.

Typography as market crier: special offers are prominently presented in glaring colours, with diagonal bars of writing and shaded backgrounds.

HAVE SCHOOL FANTASIES?
These naughty boys need textbooks to stand up in class!

GREAT ASIAN FOOD
These Asians have the biggest noodles you've ever seen!

Prison "Love" Stories- *Better to be nice than naughty!*
NYC's Times Square- *The rise and fall of America's sex capital*
Amateur Pornmaking- *An Amateur Slut Shoots Her Fuckfest Like a Pro!*
PLUS
All New Beaver Hunt
Hustler Humor
Erotic Entertainment

The application of shading, Versalia, stark colour contrasts, writing with stars, centred, or in italics, or the use of strange »Bonanza« types of font all contribute to the impression of the offered merchandise as good value to be urgently purchased and casually consumed. This impression is precisely what is intended by the operators of such sites and hence their design is effective in its own way.

Erotic content is sold differently: a well structured typographical layout in this site caters to a more upmarket target group than the pages shown above. Its name, »Sabasin«, is the name of an ancient love goddess of the Tuareg. Images are not gratuitously vulgar, and combined with a rather subtle sense of eroticism the site seems to aim predominantly at a female audience. The page has a fresh and pure quality, with its dark red background, the colour of eroticism, used in combination with a white font. The yellow font adds dynamism, warmth, and friendliness.

Übersicht
Erotikshop
Good Vibrations

4.02

Mini-screens

With restricted space, a clear structure, logic, and obvious icons are even more important than text, as there is room only for individual words. Their use should be well integrated in an overall design.

»It is only the shallow people who do not judge by appearances.«
Oscar Wilde

With mini-screens text has a secondary function. There is too little space and fonts look bad on a low-resolution pixel grid. Once the user has understood the meaning of the icon titles it is easier to follow them or their associated colour demarcation.

Font for active functions is highlighted by being overlaid on black.

Font denoting navigation fields stands out from a shaded box.

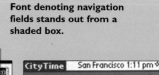

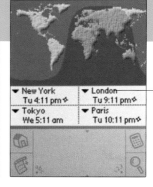

Simple font, use for brief segmer of information. Other commun tion is by visuals

Mini-screens

Space is extremely restricted on mini-screens such as mobile telephones or hand-held palmtop computers. Resolution is worse. Hence there is little use for long words and sentences. The application of logic, structure, and obvious icons, within a conclusive overall design concept to guide the user through the menu makes far more sense. Codifying words or functions by colour differentiation is one method of orientation – if a colour screen is available. Otherwise functions may be differentiated by varietions in lettering (capital or small) or the use of Versalia to distinguish menu items. Alternatively, use bar underlays for emphasis.

Small is beautiful but often detrimental to user ergonomics. With the difficulty of typing on a small screen in mind, a special simplified manu-

script alphabet is offere to help the user of the »Zire« palmtop comput

Mini-screens
: condensed information on minimal space.
Type
– use as little writing as possible.
– large font size.
– apply Versalia, underlay planes, colour to denote word (subject) hierarchies.

ΛBCDEΓGHIJ

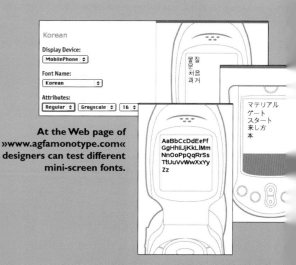

At the Web page of »www.agfamonotype.com« designers can test different mini-screen fonts.

White font to denote function.

Black font on underlay to denote choice.

Brownish red to denote non-active menu item.

Too many different colours to identify functions are confusing – preferably stick with two colours. It requires a little more effort to devise suitable hierarchies.
Left, a good example of a conclusive design application for text and colour.

Via the I-Mode you can receive sound and images on your mobile phone, e.g. current news, illustrated timetables etc.

build
your own
life

Below, Versalia marking functional items is distinguishable from mixed lettering used in complementary information.

Meta Design has devised a vivid world of colour with associated functions for the I-Mode. Here the current function bar appears in yellow and red, with the yellow font standing out from the darker tonality of red. Type for information-on-demand is easily distin-

guishable in black and dark red, against a white background. Contrast would have been too stark with the lighter colours of the function bars.

Menu items are pleasant to read in unsaturated dark red, forming an agreeable contrast with the background.

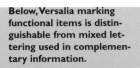

Colour to structure subject matter and writing.

Colour to structure subject matter and writing.

Leading headline as primary information: Heading, image, plus button to trigger further information on demand. The main menu is called up via a button.
Through this application of concise headings the mini-screen is kept uncluttered.

Writing is avoided almost entirely. Information is conveyed through colour.

Fonts may appear differently on different operating systems.
The following illustrations were made on an Apple Macintosh system.

5

index of typefaces which are suitable for the screen

The effect of various typefaces on screen.
Important criteria to observe when designing
appropriate typefaces for on-screen use.

5.01

118.119

Serif typefaces

Although very effective on paper, serif typefaces only look good on screen when they are very large.

»There is good and bad writing: what is inscribed in your heart and soul is good and natural, technology is depraved and artificial [...].«
Jaques Derrida

Times

on paper | 12 pt — ABCDEFGHIJKLMNOPQRSTUVWXYZ abcdefghijklmnopqrstuvwxyz 1234567890

on screen | 12 pt — ABCDEFGHIJKLMNOPQRSTUVWXYZ abcdefghijklmnopqrstuvwxyz 1234567890

14 pt | anti-aliased — ABCDEFGHIJKLMNOPQR: abcdefghijklmnopqrstuvwxyz

Walbaum

on paper | 12 pt — ABCDEFGHIJKLMNOPQRSTUVWXYZ abcdefghijklmnopqrstuvwxyz 12345

on screen | 12 pt — ABCDEFGHIJKLMNOPQRSTUVWXYZ abcdefghijklmnopqrstuvwxyz 1234567890

14 pt | anti-aliased — ABCDEFGHIJKLMNOPQ abcdefghijklmnopqrstuvw

Palatino

on paper | 12 pt — ABCDEFGHIJKLMNOPQRSTUVWXYZ abcdefghijklmnopqrstuvwxyz 12345678

on screen | 12 pt — ABCDEFGHIJKLMNOPQRSTUVWXYZ abcdefghijklmnopqrstuvwxyz 1234567890

14 pt | anti-aliased — ABCDEFGHIJKLMNOPQI abcdefghijklmnopqrstuvw.

Stone Serif

on paper | 12 pt — ABCDEFGHIJKLMNOPQRSTUVWXYZ abcdefghijklmnopqrstuvwxyz 123456

on screen | 12 pt — ABCDEFGHIJKLMNOPQRSTUVWXYZ abcdefghijklmnopqrstuvwxyz 1234567890

14 pt | anti-aliased — ABCDEFGHIJKLMNOPQ abcdefghijklmnopqrstuv

Serif typefaces

Antiqua types are characterised by their strokes of variable boldness and fine serifs. However, this makes them look untidy on screens with low resolution.

The century-old tradition in printing history of antiqua types only began to be challenged in the late nineteenth century with the advent of the two variations of the linear antiqua, with emphasised serifs or sans serifs; and lately, with new choices of appropriate typefaces for the screen. The fine differences amongst serif types become indistinguishable on screen.

Letters and serifs will get distorted by low resolution screens, so that differences in type are no longer recognisable.

The fine detail and diversity in stroke amongst antiqua types are hardly distinguishable on screen, especially with smaller sizes. Very fine hairlines might disappear altogether, and serifs appear clumped on to letters, depending on how they slot into the pixel grid.

ABC abc

Characteristics for Antiqua types: variable boldness in stroke, fine serifs.

on screen | 14 pt

ABCDEFGHIJKLMNOPQRSTUVWXYZ
abcdefghijklmnopqrstuvwxyz
1234567890

Times reads quite well on screen, contrary to other serif types, in spite of its compact width. Overall its appearance is harmonious, with a smooth flow. Its popularity (also on paper) gives Times an advantage, as it is well accepted by the readership and quickly recognised, in spite of its drawbacks on screen.

on screen | 14 pt

ABCDEFGHIJKLMNOPQRSTUVWXYZ
abcdefghijklmnopqrstuvwxyz
1234567890

The characteristic elegance of Walbaum is usually lost on screen, as its fine detail cannot be reproduced on the pixel grid. However, anti-aliased and with adequate font size an impression of its elegance may be successfully reproduced on screen.

on screen | 14 pt

ABCDEFGHIJKLMNOPQRSTUVWXYZ
abcdefghijklmnopqrstuvwxyz
1234567890

The Palatino's crispness of line and generous width support its readability. With its large punch whites it appears lighter compared to Times.

on screen | 14 pt

ABCDEFGHIJKLMNOPQRSTUVWXYZ
abcdefghijklmnopqrstuvwxyz
1234567890

Similarly to Walbaum, the Stone Serif font is unsuitable in small sizes which appear distorted on the pixel grid. Anti-aliased and in larger sizes it smoothes out to regain a semblance of its characteristic beauty.

Some other Venetians
Venetian Renaissance Antiqua
Humanistic Antiqua:

– the oldest Antiqua type
– elegance and lightness
– serifs hinged on to ground stroke in a curve
– curves along slanting axis
– small letters often with slanting ascenders
– very small contrast between thin and thick strokes
– sloping bar on the »e«

• **Centaur**
• **Weidemann**

Some other Garaldes
French Renaissance Antiqua:

– little contrast between thin and thick strokes
– curves along slanting axis
– horizontal bar on the »e«
– double decked »g«
– open »a«

• **Aldus**
• **Bembo**
• **De Roos**
• **Galliard**
• **Garamond**
• **Méridien**
• **Minion**
• **Goudy**
• **Palatino**
• **Rotis Serif**
• **Sabon**
• **Swift**
• **Trump Mediäval**
• **Vendome**

Some other Transitionals
Baroque Antiqua

– strong contrast between thin and thick strokes
– fine, often pointed serifs
– some still with curves along sloping axis

• **Baskerville**
• **Bookman**
• **Caslon**
• **Clearface**
• **Fournier**
• **Joanna**
• **Stone Serif**
• **Times**
• **Versailles**

Some other Didones
Classical Antiqua

– very strong contrast between thin and thick strokes
– very fine serifs
– curves along straight axis

• **Bodoni**
• **Century**
• **Didot**
• **Electra**
• **Monotype Modern**
• **Walbaum**

Slab serifs

The slab serifs' crudeness matches the crude resolution of the screen, so that good legibility and display can be achieved.

»Script starts with the death of the author.«
Roland Barthes

Rockwell

on paper | 12 pt	ABCDEFGHIJKLMNOPQRSTUVWXYZ abcdefghijklmnopqrstuvwxyz 123456789	
on screen | 12 pt	ABCDEFGHIJKLMNOPQRSTUVWXYZ abcdefghijklmnopqrstuvwxyz 1234567890	14 pt | anti-aliased ABCDEFGHIJKLMNOPQRS abcdefghijklmnopqrstuvw

Courier

on paper | 12 pt	ABCDEFGHIJKLMNOPQRSTUVWXYZ abcdefghijklmnopqrstuvwxyz 123456	
on screen | 12 pt	ABCDEFGHIJKLMNOPQR STUVWXYZ abcdefghijklmnopqr stuvwxyz 1234567890	14 pt | anti-aliased ABCDEFGHIJKLMNOPQRST abcdefghijklmnopqrst

Officina Serif

on paper | 12 pt	ABCDEFGHIJKLMNOPQRSTUVWXYZ abcdefghijklmnopqrstuvwxyz 1234567890	
on screen | 12 pt	ABCDEFGHIJKLMNOPQRSTUVWXYZ abcdefghijklmnopqrstuvwxyz 1234567890	14 pt | anti-aliased ABCDEFGHIJKLMNOPQRSTUVW abcdefghijklmnopqrstuvwxyz

Clarendon
Medium

on paper | 12 pt	ABCDEFGHIJKLMNOPQRSTUVWXYZ abcdefghijklmnopqrstuvwxyz 123	
on screen | 12 pt	ABCDEFGHIJKLMNOPQRSTUVWXYZ abcdefghijklmnopqrstuvwxyz 1234567890	14 pt | anti-aliased ABCDEFGHIJKLMNOPQ abcdefghijklmnopqrstuv

Slab serifs Slab or square serifs were originally conceived as emphatic types for use in encyclopaedic works. They are also useful for captions on posters and experimentally in newsprint.

Slab serifs are characterised by unvaried boldness of strokes and solid rectangular serifs, which give them a crude and basic appearance. This might be the reason for their limited appeal as reading type. However, these features make them particularly interesting for the screen: with their strong and blatant shape they will have a future on screen. Bold serifs at right angles and bold strokes reproduce well on the crude pixel grid on screen, contrary to the finer antiqua fonts.

Slab serifs with their good legibility on screen provide a good alternative to antiqua fonts.

ABC abc

Properties of slab serifs:
- unified boldness with most of the structural fonts; almost unified boldness with fonts of more classical character.
– solid, horizontal serifs
– serifs conspicuously emphasised.

---

on screen | 14 pt

ckwell

```
ABCDEFGHIJKLMNOPQRSTUVWXYZ
abcdefghijklmnopqrstuvwxyz
1234567890
```

Designed in 1934, Rockwell quickly became an American classic. It is one of the geometrical slab serifs and is distinguished by its uncompromising formal design. With its determined linearity it displays well on screen.

---

on screen | 14 pt

urier

```
ABCDEFGHIJKLMNOPQRSTUVWXYZ
abcdefghijklmnopqrstuvwxyz
1234567890
```

On screen, Courier provides a viable alternative to Antiqua types. Its open minuscules make it especially easy to read in small sizes.

---

on screen | 14 pt

icina Serif

```
ABCDEFGHIJKLMNOPQRSTUVWXYZ
abcdefghijklmnopqrstuvwxyz
1234567890
```

An elegant slab serif type is provided by the Officina Serif with its compact width, a result of its vertical weight. Hence not easily legible in small sizes, and should only be applied in large sizes.

---

on screen | 14 pt

rendon ium

```
ABCDEFGHIJKLMNOPQRSTUVWXYZ
abcdefghijklm nopqrstuvwxyz
1234567890
```

Clarendon is close to many classical Antiqua types. Its beautifully varied boldness is lost completely on screen, but due to its generous width it is easy to read. Increasing the boldness will underline the unifying linear tendency.

Slab Serifs
With classical character:

– Egyptiennes based on classical fonts (e.g. Bodoni). Very little difference between Antiqua and Egyptienne
– strong serifs, sometimes with blatant emphasis
– some variation in boldness
– solid, strong shapes

Slab Serifs
With structural character:

– strong serifs
– serifs attached horizontally
– little variation in boldness

Some other Slab Serifs
Egyptienne, Square Serif

• **Caecilia**
• **Cheltenham**
• **Egizio**
• **Egyptian**
• **Excelsior**
• **Glypha**
• **Impressum**
• **LinoLetter**
• **Lubalin Graph**
• **Lucida Typewriter**
• **Memphis**
• **ITC Officina Serif**
• **Osiris**
• **Serifa**

Clarendon Rg

Glypha Rg

Lineales |
Neo-Grotesque

The neo-grotesque Lineales types reproduce very well on screen.

»[It] should match the technically designed forms
of cars and planes,
based on a functional visual appearance,
without decoration and gimmicks.«
László Moholy-Nagy about modern typography

Helvetica

on paper | 12 pt
ABCDEFGHIJKLMNOPQRSTUVWXYZ abcdefghijklmnopqrstuvwxyz 123456789

on screen | 12 pt
ABCDEFGHIJKLMNOPQRSTUVWXYZ
abcdefghijklmnopqrstuvwxyz
1234567890

14 pt | anti-aliased
ABCDEFGHIJKLMNOPQR
abcdefghijklmnopqrstuvwx

Helvetica 63
Medium Extended

on paper | 12 pt
ABCDEFGHIJKLMNOPQRSTUVWXYZ abcdefghijklmnopqrstuvw

on screen | 12 pt
ABCDEFGHIJKLMNOPQRSTUVWXYZ
abcdefghijklmnopqrstuvwxyz
1234567890

14 pt | anti-aliased
ABCDEFGHIJKLMNO
abcdefghijklmnopqrs

Univers

on paper | 12 pt
ABCDEFGHIJKLMNOPQRSTUVWXYZ abcdefghijklmnopqrstuvwxyz 123456

on screen | 12 pt
ABCDEFGHIJKLMNOPQRSTUVWXYZ
abcdefghijklmnopqrstuvwxyz
1234567890

14 pt | anti-aliased
ABCDEFGHIJKLMNOPQF
abcdefghijklmnopqrstuvv

Akzidenz Grotesk

on paper | 12 pt
ABCDEFGHIJKLMNOPQRSTUVWXYZ abcdefghijklmnopqrstuvwxyz 1234567890

on screen | 12 pt
ABCDEFGHIJKLMNOPQRSTUVWXYZ
abcdefghijklmnopqrstuvwxyz
1234567890

14 pt | anti-aliased
ABCDEFGHIJKLMNOPQF
abcdefghijklmnopqrstuvwxy

**Lineales
Neo-Grotesques**

The neo-grotesque sans serif types are characterised by their uniform boldness and the absence of serifs.
Unspectacular and uniform in appearance they always leave a good impression on screen, contrary to their humanist and geometrical sisters, whose impact on screen should always be carefully assessed in advance.
Contrary to Antiqua types, statutory standardisation such as the DIN norm does not include categories of stylistic differentiation for sans serif types. The designer has to rely on his own experience.

Neo-grotesques are preferable to humanist or geometrical sans serif types. The designer should have some experience with the impact of these kinds of Lineales, as there is no statutory classification available (c.f. list on the right).

ABC abc

Arial

Properties for Lineales (Neo-Grotesque):
– nearly uniform boldness.
– no serifs.

on screen | 14 pt

vetica

ABCDEFGHIJKLMNOPQRSTUVWXYZ
abcdefghijklmnopqrstuvwxyz
1234567890

Even on screen Helvetica has become a classic. In spite of its compact width which makes it so economical to use it reads well on screen, due to its elevated x-height.

on screen | 14 pt

vetica 65
dium Extended

ABCDEFGHIJKLMNOPQRSTUVWXYZ
abcdefghijklmnopqrstuvwxyz
1234567890

One good variety is Helvetica Medium Extended, though in need of wider spacing for enhanced legibility.

on screen | 14 pt

ivers

ABCDEFGHIJKLMNOPQRSTUVWXYZ
abcdefghijklmnopqrstuvwxyz
1234567890

Another favourable variation on Helvetica is provided by Univers. Its sober appearance is particularly advantageous for use in larger sizes.

on screen | 14 pt

idenz Grotesk

ABCDEFGHIJKLMNOPQRSTUVWXYZ
abcdefghijklmnopqrstuvwxyz
1234567890

One of the oldest Grotesques, Akzidenz Grotesk, was designed long before the computer age in 1896. It reads surprisingly well on screen due to its unpretentious and determined shape.

It can be enhanced with some extra spacing.

DIN classification of types
(DIN 16518 from 1964, after Maximilian Vox)

I	**Venetian Renaissance Antiqua** (Humanist, i.e. Centaur)
II	**French Renaissance Antiqua** (Garalde, i.e. Garamond)
III	**Baroque Antiqua** (Réale, i.e. Baskerville)
IV	**Classical Antiqua** (Didone, i.e. Bodoni)
V	**Slab Serif** (Mécane, i.e. Clarendon)
VI	**Linear Antiqua sans serif** (Linéale, i.e. Helvetica)
VII	**Antiqua-variations** (Incise, i.e. Profil)
VIII	**Cursive Scripts** (Scripte, i.e. Mistral)
IX	**Cursive Antiqua** (Manuaire, i.e. Polka)
X	**Black letters, Fraktur, gothic types** (i.e. Unger Fraktur)

Lineales
Neo-grotesque
With classical character:

– sans serifs
– nearly uniform boldness
– sober overall impression

Lineales
Neo-grotesque
With classical character:

- **Akzidenz Grotesk**
- **Arial**
- **Corporate S**
- **Folio**
- **Grotesque**
- **Helvetica**
- **Univers**
- **Venus**

Lineales
Sans Serif, Gothic, Antique, Grotesque

5.03

124.125

Lineales |
Humanists and
Geometrics

The Humanist and Geometric varieties of Lineales
should not be used indiscriminately in comparision to
the Lineales with classical character.

»It is the duty of a type not to draw attention to itself.«
Ian Tschichold

Gill Sans

on paper | 12 pt

ABCDEFGHIJKLMNOPQRSTUVWXYZ abcdefghijklmnopqrstuvwxyz 1234567890

on screen | 12 pt

ABCDEFGHIJKLMNOPQRSTUVWXYZ
abcd efghijklmnopqrstuvwxyz
1234567890

14 pt | anti-aliased

ABCDEFGHIJKLMNOPQRST
abcdefghijklmnopqrstuvwxyz

Frutiger

on paper | 12 pt

ABCDEFGHIJKLMNOPQRSTUVWXYZ abcdefghijklmnopqrstuvwxyz 123456789

on screen | 12 pt

ABCDEFGHIJKLMNOPQRSTUVWXYZ
abcd efghijklmnopqrstuvwxyz
1234567890

14 pt | anti-aliased

ABCDEFGHIJKLMNOPQRS
abcdefghijklmnopqrstuvw

Eurostile

on paper | 12 pt

ABCDEFGHIJKLMNOPQRSTUVWXYZ abcdefghijklmnopqrstuvwxyz 123456

on screen | 12 pt

ABCDEFGHIJKLMNOPQRSTUVWXYZ
abcdefghijklmnopqrstuvwxyz
1234567890

14 pt | anti-aliased

ABCDEFGHIJKLMNOPQR
abcdefghijklmnopqrstuvw

Futura

on paper | 12 pt

ABCDEFGHIJKLMNOPQRSTUVWXYZ abcdefghijklmnopqrstuvwxyz 1234567890

on screen | 12 pt

ABCDEFGHIJKLMNOPQRSTUVWXYZ
abcdefghijklmnopqrstuvwxyz
1234567890

14 pt | anti-aliased

ABCDEFGHIJKLMNOPQRS
abcdefghijklmnopqrstuvw

**Lineales
Humanists and Geometrics**

Geometric sans serif types are characterised by
their uniform boldness, an absence of serifs, and
a structure based on geometrical shapes. They
leave an impression that is highly aesthetic but
has a detrimental effect on legibility. Characters
are designed as singular entities with little
consideration for contact with their adjacent
neighbour.
Due to large punch whites they show up distinctly
on screen, but with their disregard for smooth
successions of characters they should only be
applied to short sentences or captions.

Humanist sans serif types are characterised by
variable boldness derived from Renaissance
types, and again the absence of serifs.
The fine variations in boldness which look
so appealing and elegant on paper are lost
completely on screen.

**Not all sans serif types
have equally advantageous
properties of legibility
on screen.
The Humanist and
Geometric varieties
should be carefully
assessed in advance
of their planned
application.**

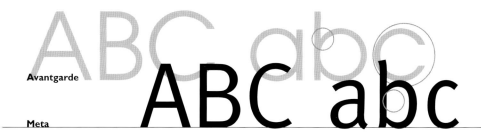

Avantgarde

Meta

ABC abc

Properties for sans serif types:
Humanists are sans serif types, although with variable boldness.

Geometrics use uniformly bold strokes, and they are more structural in appearance and derived from basic geometric shapes.

Sans

on screen | 14 pt

ABCDEFGHIJKLMNOPQRSTUVWXYZ
abcdefghijklmnopqrstuvwxyz
1234567890

Gill Sans is characterised by large and simple characters that stand in good relation to one another. Compared to other geometric sans serif types with solitary characters Gill Sans can be read well. The characteristic varia-

tions in boldness do not translate on screen.

tiger

on screen | 14 pt

ABCDEFGHIJKLMNOPQRSTUVWXYZ
abcdefghijklmnopqrstuvwxyz
1234567890

Frutiger is characterised by undulating curvatures derived from typewriter scripts. These are utterly lost on screen, especially in smaller sizes. When this is not a deterrent,

it can nonetheless be read well on screen.

ostile

on screen | 14 pt

ABCDEFGHIJKLMNOPQRSTUVWXYZ
abcdefghijklmnopqrstuvwxyz
1234567890

Eurostile is a geometric sans serif type with predominantly square shapes. Its square appearance and large punch whites translate very well into clear screen legibility. For longer text passages other fonts

are preferable though, as the familiar solitary nature of the characters has a detrimental effect on legibility.

ura

on screen | 14 pt

ABCDEFGHIJKLMNOPQRSTUVWXYZ
abcdefghijklmnopqrstuvwxyz
1234567890

Like Eurostile, Futura is another geometric sans serif type, this time based on the circle. Characters with large punch whites aid the legibility of phrases, but, as with Eurostile, it is not recommended for use in long text passages.

Lineales
Humanists
With Renaissance attributes:

– basic shapes derived from Renaissance Antiqua types
– variable boldness
– horizontal direction and good succession of characters attaining conclusive representation for phrases.
– usually with double-decker »g«
– open »a«

Lineales
Humanists
With Renaissance attributes:

• **Formata**
• **Frutiger**
• **Gill Sans**
• **Goudy Sans**
• **Legacy Sans**
• **Lucida Sans**
• **Maxima**
• **Meta**
• **Optima**
• **Rotis Sans**
• **Scala Sans**
• **Stone Sans**
• **Syntax**
• **TheSans**
• **Today**

Lineales
Geometric
With structural attributes:

– derived from basic geometric shapes such as the circle, square, and rectangle
– solitary appearance of individual characters with little relation to adjacent letters with detrimental effect on legibility

Lineales
Geometric
With structural attributes:

• **Avantgarde**
• **Bauhaus**
• **Eurostile**
• **Futura**
• **Kabel**

Lineales
Sans Serif, Gothic, Antique, Grotesque

Bauhaus

oRG

ag

Optima

5.04

Screen fonts |
Pixel fonts

Usually fonts for the screen are designed as sans serifs, with large x-heights and generous widths.
Pixel fonts for short words as used in buttons usually consist of capital letters only for better reproduction in small sizes.

»Good typography has to be perfectly legible and, as such, the result of intelligent planning.«
Jan Tschichold

Verdana	on paper | 12 pt	ABCDEFGHIJKLMNOPQRSTUVWXYZ abcdefghijklmnopqrstuvwxyz 1234
	on screen | 12 pt	ABCDEFGHIJKLMNOPQRSTUVWXYZ abcdefghijklmnopqrstuvwxyz 1234567890
		14 pt | anti-aliased ABCDEFGHIJKLMNOPQF abcdefghijklmnopqrstu

Tahoma	on paper | 12 pt	ABCDEFGHIJKLMNOPQRSTUVWXYZ abcdefghijklmnopqrstuvwxyz 1234567890
	on screen | 12 pt	ABCDEFGHIJKLMNOPQRSTUVWXYZ abcdefghijklmnopqrstuvwxyz 1234567890
		14 pt | anti-aliased ABCDEFGHIJKLMNOPQRST abcdefghijklmnopqrstuvwx

Geneva	on paper | 12 pt	ABCDEFGHIJKLMNOPQRSTUVWXYZ abcdefghijklmnopqrstuvwxyz 123456
	on screen | 12 pt	ABCDEFGHIJKLMNOPQRSTUVWXYZ abcdefghijklmnopqrstuvwxyz 1234567890
		14 pt | anti-aliased ABCDEFGHIJKLMNOPQRS abcdefghijklmnopqrstuv

Trebuchet MS	on paper | 12 pt	ABCDEFGHIJKLMNOPQRSTUVWXYZ abcdefghijklmnopqrstuvwxyz 1234567890
	on screen | 12 pt	ABCDEFGHIJKLMNOPQRSTUVWXYZ abcdefghijklmnopqrstuvwxyz 1234567890
		14 pt | anti-aliased ABCDEFGHIJKLMNOPQRST abcdefghijklmnopqrstuvw

Computer fonts provide solutions to problems of screen display. Even in small sizes (e.g. 10 pt) they still read well, which conventional type cannot achieve.

Screen fonts

Screen fonts are designed specifically for screen use and are able to compensate for limitations such as bad resolution. Even for small sizes legibility is good.

Typeface is less precise than in conventional script. Fine detail and differentiation of boldness of character strokes are omitted, as they cannot be reproduced on screen. The x-height is exaggerated to give minuscules a larger appearance for improved readability. These fonts are characterised by their generous widths and bigger punch whites, due also to increased gaps between letters.

Often screen fonts have a balanced appearance only as long as they remain aliased, as their shape has been specifically adapted for the screen's pixel grid. This applies especially to diagonals, curves, and roundels. These fonts have been designed on the computer, as opposed to conventional scripts which have been drafted, often freehand, by brush or pen and nib.

Pixel fonts

Pixel fonts which have to be read in tiny sizes on restricted spaces such as buttons for navigation or captions usually consist of capital letters only. They are available in one size only, ranging between 5 and 9 pt, which is the minimum requirement for reproduction on screen. Pixel fonts have been ideally adapted for the pixel grid and cannot be anti-aliased due to their tiny size and the lack of available pixels: punch whites would merge into dark spaces. These small pixel fonts are unsuitable for longer portions of text, but they do provide an excellent solution to any spatial constraints.

ABC abc

Verdana

Screen font characteristics:
– large x-heights and
  usually sans serifs.
– unified boldness of
  stroke, characters with
big punch whites giving
rise to generous widths.

on screen	14 pt

ABCDEFGHIJKLMNOPQRSTUVWXYZ
abcdefghijklmnopqrstuvwxyz
1234567890

For its pleasant legibility, Verdana has become one of the most successful fonts on screen. Its characters are individual for ease of distinction (viz. Minuscule l and capital I). Verdana is further equipped with wide punch whites and generous widths.

on screen	14 pt

ABCDEFGHIJKLMNOPQRSTUVWXYZ
abcdefghijklmnopqrstuvwxyz
1234567890

Tahoma was devised by the same man as Verdana, Matthew Carter, with evident similarities between them. Tohama is less generous in width, therefore it is not as legible as Verdana.

on screen	14 pt

ABCDEFGHIJKLMNOPQRSTUVWXYZ
abcdefghijklmnopqrstuvwxyz
1234567890

Another font with good legibility on screen is Geneva, a system font for Apple Macintosh. Its structure is based on rectangular shapes with slim letters which are spaced well apart for ease of distinction.

on screen	14 pt

ABCDEFGHIJKLMNOPQRSTUVWXYZ
abcdefghijklmnopqrstuvwxyz
1234567890

Trebuchet appears smaller than the above typefaces, due to its reduced x-height. Letter shapes are rounded and more complex than with Verdana. Though not particularly good to read it has much better legibility than conventional type.

Pixel fonts
Pixel fonts are designed for short sentences or single words for buttons, captions and other navigational devices.

– mostly no lower case
  characters
– one size only (5–9 pt)
– usable for very small sizes
– unsuitable for anti-aliasing

Some pixel fonts

- **Binary**
- **Hilogin**
- **Mini 7**
- **MiniSerif**
- **Rotorkeff**
- **Silkscreen**
- **SkinnyMini**

Screen fonts
Optimum legibility for screen resolution:

– high x-height gives large
  appearance to characters
– unified boldness of stroke
– big punch whites and
  generous widths
– sans serifs; any serifs are
  adapted to the pixel grid

Some screen fonts

- **Chicago**
- **Espy Sans**
- **Geneva**
- **Georgia**
- **Monaco**
- **Nina**
- **New York**
- **Tahoma**
- **Tiresias**
- **Trebuchet MS**
- **Truth**
- **Verdana**

MINI 7   ABCDE

MINI 7 TIGHT   ABCDE

MINI 7 BOLD   **ABCD**

MINI 7 CONDENSED   ABCDE

MINI 7 BOLD CONDENSED   **ABCD.**

Screen fonts |
Serifs and sans serifs

There are now serif fonts with excellent qualities of legibility as viable alternatives to Grotesque fonts. The introduction of restrained serifs holds the eye on the line.

»Typography fostered the modern idea of individuality, but it destroyed the medieval sense of community and integration.«
Neil Postman

Chicago	on paper | 12 pt	ABCDEFGHIJKLMNOPQRSTUVWXYZ abcdefghijklmnopqrstuvwxyz 1
	on screen | 12 pt	ABCDEFGHIJKLMNOPQRSTUVWXYZ abcdefghijklmnopqrstuvwxyz 1234567890
	14 pt | anti-aliased	ABCDEFGHIJKLMNOPQR abcdefghijklmnopqrs
Monaco	on paper | 12 pt	ABCDEFGHIJKLMNOPQRSTUVWXYZ abcdefghijklmnopqrstuvwxyz 1234567
	on screen | 12 pt	ABCDEFGHIJKLMNOPQRSTUVWXYZ abcdefghijklmnopqrstuvwxyz 1234567890
	14 pt | anti-aliased	ABCDEFGHIJKLMNOPQRST abcdefghijklmnopqrst
Georgia	on paper | 12 pt	ABCDEFGHIJKLMNOPQRSTUVWXYZ abcdefghijklmnopqrstuvwxyz 12345678
	on screen | 12 pt	ABCDEFGHIJKLMNOPQRSTUVWXYZ abcdefghijklmnopqrstuvwxyz 1234567890
	14 pt | anti-aliased	ABCDEFGHIJKLMNOPQ abcdefghijklmnopqrstuvw
New York	on paper | 12 pt	ABCDEFGHIJKLMNOPQRSTUVWXYZ abcdefghijklmnopqrstuvwxyz 12
	on screen | 12 pt	ABCDEFGHIJKLMNOPQRSTUVWXYZ abcdefghijklmnopqrstuvwxyz 1234567890
	14 pt | anti-aliased	ABCDEFGHIJKLMNOPQ abcdefghijklmnopqrst

Screen fonts
Most screen fonts come without serifs. However, some alternative serif types have been developed for screen applications. Their serifs are less fine than in traditional Antiqua types, and have been designed to fit the pixel grid and show up better on screen. Here serifs appear selectively and might be missing altogether in some characters. They occur only when needed to provide visual guidance.

Screen fonts have been devised specifically for screen applications. Often they look crude on paper.

Fonts often appear differently depending on the operating system used, and their definition on screen may also vary with size. Therefore all available options should always be tested first.

ABC

ABC abc

		Properties of serif screen fonts:	– fewer serifs.
		– serifs designed for integration with pixel grid.	– increased x-height.

Georgia

on screen | 14 pt	ABCDEFGHIJKLMNOPQRSTUVWXYZ abcdefghijklmnopqrstuvwxyz 1234567890	The mechanical precision of Chicago is not particularly appealing visually, but its legibility is good especially with smaller sizes. Based on rectangular shapes, it moulds well in a pixel grid.	Anti-aliased, its legibility is destroyed.

cago

on screen | 14 pt	ABCDEFGHIJKLMNOPQRSTUVWXYZ abcdefghijklmnopqrstuvwxyz 1234567890	Monaco, too, has excellent legibility for smaller sizes. It is a sans serif font, where the perception of the minuscule »i«, the minuscule »l« and the digit »1« is improved by the addition of serifs, which also helps	to avoid confusion between them.

naco

on screen | 14 pt	ABCDEFGHIJKLMNOPQRSTUVWXYZ abodefghijklmnopqrstuvwxyz 1234567890	Georgia is another serif font developed for the screen. Serifs have been simplified and occur only where appropriate to maintain visual attention on a line. A special feature about this very legible font	are its median digits which have ascenders and descenders like minuscules.

orgia

on screen | 14 pt	ABCDEFGHIJKLMNOPQRSTUVWXYZ abcdefghijklmnopqrstuvwxyz 1234567890	Another serif font specifically designed for the screen is New York. It stands out for its elevated x-heights that define its legibility. The structure of the serifs with New York is finer than in Georgia.	

v York

Many typefaces from an era before the advent of the computer have since been altered and adapted for improved display on screen. This has been achieved by increasing x-heights and making strokes bolder.

Pre-installed fonts with respective equivalents in Mac and PC:

Mac Fonts	PC Fonts
Helvetica	Arial
Times	Times New Roman
Courier	Courier New
Symbol	Symbol
Geneva	MS Sans Serif
New York	MS Serif
Chicago	-
Zapf Dingbats	WingDings

Some Screen fonts
With serifs:

– based on traditional Antiqua types, but with simplified serifs
– horizontal serifs to provide visual guidance

• Georgia
• New York

Screen fonts

Minion

Minion Web

5.05

Other classifications

The types categorised under **DIN VII–X**, and a number of the latest experimental typefaces are of little value on screen, unless used in very large sizes.
Their suitability depends on the objectives of the task at hand.

»Whatever you occupy yourself with,
you will always find beauty in what is good and usefu
Baldassare Castigli

OCR A

on paper | 12 pt ABCDEFGHIJKLMNOPQRSTUVWXYZ abcdefghijklmnopqrstuvwxyz 123

on screen | 12 pt
ABCDEFGHIJKLMNOPQRSTUVWXYZ
abcdefghijklmnopqrstuvwxyz
1234567890

14 pt | anti-aliased
ABCDEFGHIJKLMNOPQ
abcdefghijklmnopc

Trixie Plain

on paper | 12 pt ABCDEFGHIJKLMNOPQRSTUVWXYZ abcdefghijklmnopqrstuvwxyz 1234567890

on screen | 12 pt
ABCDEFGHIJKLMNOPQRSTUVWXYZ
abcdefghijklmnopqrstuvwxyz
1234567890

14 pt | anti-aliased
ABCDEFGHIJKLMNOPQRSTU
abcdefghijklmnopqrstuv

Erikrighthand

on paper | 12 pt ABCDEFGHIJKLMNOPQRSTUVWXYZ abcdefghijklmnopqrstuvwxyz 1234567890

on screen | 12 pt
ABCDEFGHIJKLMNOPQRSTUVWXYZ
abcdefghijklmnopqrstuvwxyz
1234567890

14 pt | anti-aliased
ABCDEFGHIJKLMNOPQRSTUVWXYZ
abcdefghijklmnopqrstuvwxyz

Old English Text

on paper | 12 pt ABCDEFGHIJKLMNOPQRSTUVWXYZ abcdefghijklmnopqrstuvwxyz 123456

on screen | 12 pt
ABCDEFGHIJKLMNOPQRSTUVWXYZ
abcdefghijklmnopqrstuvwxyz
1234567890

14 pt | anti-aliased
ABCDEFGHIJKLMNC
abcdefghijklmnopqrstuvwxyz

Other classifications

Certain Antiqua varieties should only be used after careful deliberation, and their application requires great sensibility. Amongst them are Antiqua varieties (DIN 16518, group VII – decorative Antiqua types not classified under groups I–VI, e.g. Codex), cursive types (DIN 16518, group VIII, e.g. Mistral), cursive Antiquas (DIN 16518, group IX, types derived from Antiquas and their cursive varieties and altered to resemble traits of individual hand-writing, e.g. Polka), Gothic types (DIN 16518, group VII, e.g. Old Schwabach), or very recent experimental types. If you must use them, it is only recommended to do so in very large sizes and anti-aliased.

Apart from poor legibility on low resolution screens, another drawback of some lesser known serif or sans serif types lies with their unfamiliarity. Please observe at all times: »What you know, you read best.«

Angst  **Beowolf** ABC abc   **Emigre Ten** ABC abc

ABCabc

Sand

Many experimental types are not linked by any common categories. However, they are all distinctly individual.

OCR A | on screen | 14 pt

ABCDEFGHIJKLMNOPQRSTUVWXYZ
abcdefghijklmnopqrstuvwxyz
1234567890

OCR A was one of the first types to be developed for computer applications. However, it was originally conceived for automatic computer readability, and not for legibility by the human eye. It is a proportional type where the characters are all apportioned equal space, hence its somewhat rugged appearance. But characters are easily distinguishable.

Trixie Plain | on screen | 14 pt

ABCDEFGHIJKLMNOPQRSTUVWXYZ
abcdefghijklmnopqrstuvwxyz
1234567890

Trixie is an amorphous version of Courier. In their ruined state its classical characters look quite appealing. Never to be used in small sizes on screen and always anti-aliased. Otherwise it will appear severed and unintelligible on screen.

Erikrighthand | on screen | 14 pt

ABCDEFGHIJKLMNOPQRSTUVWXYZ
abcdefghijklmnopqrstuvwxyz
1234567890

Erikrighthand is one of the types resembling the traits of spontaneous handwriting. It is utterly useless on screen: its diagonals and curvatures do not reproduce well and tend to get torn apart, furthermore the viewer is challenged to become familiarised with an unconventional type.

Old English Text | on screen | 14 pt

ABCDEFGHIJKLMNOPQRSTUVWXYZ
abcdefghijklmnopqrstuvwxyz
1234567890

Old English belongs to the gothic types. Similar drawbacks apply as for cursive types. Additionally, its characteristic fine lines reproduce poorly.

No classification
Many more recent types are so different that they defy classification:

- **Angst**
- **Emigre Ten**
- **New Alphabet**
- **Template Gothic**
- **OCR A**

Angst

Antiqua Varianten
Incise (DIN 16518/VII)
Antiqua types defying categorisation under DIN 16518, classes I–VI

– decorative or monumental expression

- **Codex**
- **Columna**
- **Largo**
- **Neuland**
- **Profil**
- **Stop**

Codex

Cursive scripts
Scripte (DIN 16518/VIII)
Cursive types are printing-type versions of traditional Latin cursive scripts for school or clerical use

– resemble handwritten script by fountain pen or brush; curvilinear
– spontaneous or festive appearance
– link lines for minuscules

- **Edwardian Script**
- **Erikleft/righthand**
- **Lithographia**
- **Mistral**

Mistral

Edwardian Script

Cursive Antiqua
Manuaire (DIN 16518/IX)
Types derived from Antiqua or cursive varieties; characters adapted to resemble handwriting

– without link lines, unlike cursive types
– vertical orientation of characters

- **Hyperion**
- **Polka**
- **Tekton**
- **Time Script**

Polka

Gothic types
German types (DIN 16518/X/a–e)
Very old type resembling inscriptions by broad quill

– fractured curves
– strong contrast between bold and fine line
– fine inceptional up-stroke and terminal strokes

- **Alte Schwabacher**
- **Caslon Gotisch**
- **Fette Fraktur**
- **Koch-Kurrent**
- **Old English Text**
- **Unger Fraktur**

Alte Schwabacher

5.06

Non-Latin scripts |
Asian scripts

Because of their complexity Chinese and Japanese scripts are difficult to display on screen. They need to appear large in order not to appear untidy, cluttered, or lumped.
The structured appearance of Korean script makes it almost ideal for on-screen adaptation.

»By the spring breezes,
the beautiful girl is pushed.
What indignity!«
Gyōtai

Chinese
traditional

on screen | Monotype Bei

蒙納優質中文字庫

Chinese
symplified

on screen | C Yuen

蒙纳优质中文字库

Japanese

on screen | HG Gothic

印象あざやかな書体とデザイン
印象あざやかな書体とデザイン

Korean

on screen | Hy Gothic

아름다운 한글 글꼴의 표현
아름다운 한글 글꼴의 표현

Asian Asian scripts are based on the concept of an invisible rectangular frame in which the strokes are arranged. However, complexity and formal appearance of strokes may differ widely. Chinese or Japanese are very close to their calligraphic roots and are extremely complex in the number of strokes and their formal arrangement. Beautiful to behold, they are nonetheless difficult to display on low resolution screens when the letters get too small. When letters in small font sizes are anti-aliased, relevant detail will be clumped up. There is a similar effect especially with Chinese, when fonts are emphasised too boldly. Therefore comparatively large font sizes should be chosen. Bold emphasis and anti-aliasing only make sense with very large characters, especially with traditional Chinese script.
Less care is necessary with Korean script with its unified and restful appearance due to its structural character. Strokes are spaced well apart for ease of distinction. Usually they are arranged horizontally or vertically without too many curves. The script adapts very well to the orthogonal pixel grid of the electronic screen and is hence easy to take in even in rather small sizes.

on screen | C Hei

nese
ditional

蒙納優質中文字
蒙納優質中文字
蒙納優

Traditional Chinese script is still used today in Taiwan and by many Chinese expatriate communities worldwide.
There are eight basic strokes with Chinese script, which form the basis of each character. The complex arrangement is contained in an imaginary rectangle.

on screen | Monotype Hei

nese
plified

蒙纳优质中文字库
蒙纳优质中文字库

The government of the People's Republic of China simplified the traditional Chinese script between 1950 and 1960. This version is used in modern-day China and in Singapore. Simplified Chinese script looks much more open and uncluttered, and is far more appropriate for the screen than the complex traditional script with its calligraphic trappings.

on screen | HG Maru Gothic

anese

印象あざやかな書体とデ
印象あざやかな書体とデ

Its calligraphic roots are clearly evident in Japanese script and many characters are extremely complex. This can be detrimental to the legibility on screen, especially when smaller font sizes are anti-aliased. It is recommended to display Japanese characters in adequately large font sizes.

on screen | Hy Graphic

ean

아름다운 한글 글꼴
아름다운 한글 글꼴

Of all the Asiatic scripts mentioned the Korean script is best suited for on-screen display.
It has an open appearance with strokes arranged in an uncluttered fashion. Their vertical and horizontal distribution with very few curving lines is not only aesthetically pleasing but also easy to display on screen.

Chinese

Chinese script is among the oldest known to humankind. During the many thousands of years of its history many developments and alterations have taken place.
In its modern form Chinese goes back to about 100 B.C., when Xu Shan composed the first dictionary of the Chinese language, using approximately 9.500 characters. Modern-day Chinese script is an amalgamation of pictograms, ideograms of inherent semantic and phonetic connotations, and is derived from a tradition of calligraphic painting recurringly simplified and standardised into today's form.

Japanese | Amalgamation

Japanese is an amalgamation of three writing systems: Kanji, Hiragana, and Katakana, the latter being termed Kana.
Kanji is used to denote Names, nouns and verbs and is based on Chinese characters, contrary to Kana, which is based on a syllabic system. Knowledge of about 2000 characters of Kanji is required for daily use.
Kana started evolving in the 9th century A.D. and was formally regulated around 1900, and it is sufficient for writing a Japanese text. However, as the use of spaces is unknown in Japanese and word-wrap can be arbitrary, the application of the mixed scripts makes individual phrases easier to distinguish. Kana characters are simplified versions of Kanji and are made up of a maximum of six strokes. The Hiragana with their predominantly curved appearance are used mainly as reflexives and grammatical elements and may sometimes denote an old-fashioned Kanji. Katakana, with their rectilinear appearance are used mainly to denote names and foreign expressions.

Korean | Amalgamation

Korean also consists of two systems of writing, Hanja, based on Chinese characters, and Hangul, a syllabic system that came into existence under the rule of King Seyong. Hangul has only found widespread application in the 20th century and still has not completely displaced Hanja and the prestige associated with the ancient Chinese characters. Though Hangul has been acclaimed as a perfect writing system. Graphically, the characters are contained within an imaginary rectangular frame as in Chinese. Through the predominantly horizontal arrangement of strokes the aesthetic impact of the script is highly sophisticated. Today Korean is written mainly in Hangul with a splattering of individual Hanja expressions.

Guli

文字库

Hy GungSo

글꼴의

TB Classic Mincho

5.06

Non-Latin scripts |
Cyrillic
Hebrew
Greek

Cyrillic, Greek, and Hebrew scripts are linked by strong geometry, a common sense of proportion, and a constructed effect, which makes them easy to adapt for on-screen use.

»Yet, as much as she admired the carrier of beauty, she saw him only as a poor remedy for the worst of pains.«
Plato

Cyrillic

on screen | Arial Cyrillic

АБВГДЕЖЗИЙКЛМНОП
РСТУФХЦЧШЩЪЫЬЭЮЯ
ЂЃЄЉЊЋЌЎЏ
абвгдежзийклмнопрстуфхцч
шщъыьэюяђѓєљњћќўџ

Courier Cyrillic

АБВГДЕЖЗИЙКЛ
абвгдежзийклм

Greek

on screen | Arial Greek
normal

ΑΒΓΔΕΖΗ
ΘΙΚΛΜΝΞ
ΟΠΡΣΤΥΦ
ΧΨΩΑΒΓΔ

αβγδεζηθικ
λμνξοπρστ
υφχψωςαβ

Arial Greek
bold

ΑΒΓΔΕΖΗ
ΘΙΚΛΜΝΞ
αβγδεζηθι

Hebrew

on screen | Arial Hebrew

מסה זו היא פרי שנים רבות של פעילות מ
מסה זו היא פרי שנים רבות של פעילות

Alachsone

ס רבות של פע
נים רבות של פ

Cyrillic, Greek and Hebrew Capital letters in Cyrillic and Greek scripts, both obviously of the same origin, have a similar aesthetically sophisticated and strong, geometric impact. For these scripts fonts originally developed for Latin scripts, such as Times, Arial, or Helvetica (Lagoda in Russian) are now available. Similar rules as for Latin scripts apply: serif fonts are less appropriate for on-screen use than Grotesque fonts. This is less necessary for the representation of capital letters, but more for the minuscules whose fine detail quickly becomes indistinguishable on screen with a serif type.

In Hebrew script capital letters have a similarly strong impact. When adapting the script to screen, the use of italicised fonts should be avoided, unless you use very large sizes. Its upright lettering, uncluttered appearance, and orthogonal structure makes Hebrew script particularly suitable for displaying text for ease of intake.

on screen | Times Cyrillic	АБВГДЕЖЗИЙКЛМНОП РСТУФХЦЧШЩЪЬЬЭЮЯ ЋГСЉЊЂКЎЏΓ абвгдежзийклмнопрстуфхцч шщъььэюяħѓсљњ ħќўџг		Cyrillic script has a similar, strongly geometric structure to its ancestor ancient Greek, especially the solidly built capital letters. Many fonts that were originally developed for Latin scripts are now available for it.	As in Latin scripts, serif type fonts look more cluttered than grotesque types.
on screen | Rockwell Greek	ΑΒΓΔΕΖΗ ΘΙΚΛΜΝΞ ΟΠΡΣΤΥΦ αβγδεζηθικ λμνξοπρστ	Times Greek ΑΒΓΔΕΖΗ ΘΙΚΛΜΝ ΞΟΠΡΣΤΥ αβγδεζηθικ λμνξοπρστ	In Greek script, capital letters appear austere and with a strong aesthetic impact derived from their geometric structure, which makes them well distinguishable on screen. As the appearance of the	minuscules is less powerful they require larger sizes and a sensible choice of font, just as with Latin script. Again, grotesque fonts are more suitable than serif fonts.
on screen | Levenim	מסה זו היא פרי שנים רבות של פעילו מסה זו היא פרי שנים רבות של פעי		Hebrew scripts are extremely suitable for use on screen, as long as italicised fonts are avoided. The notion of the script's rigid appearance (an excuse by some to abet the linguistic segregation of Jews) may derive from its austere character and solidly square structure. With its characteristic absence of ornamentation and complexity, and with its orthogonal strokes this	script is particularly well suited for containment in the pixel grid. There is not much the designer can improve, as long as italicised fonts are avoided.

Cyrillic

Old Cyrillic was developed from ancient Greek script by Saint Cyril in the mid 9th century A.D., maintaining the succession of the alphabet and a similar formal appearance. Tsar Peter the Great reformed the script by abandoning superfluous letters and introducing missing new ones. Not even its formal appearance was spared and the script was made to resemble Latin script more closely. Cyrillic was reformed again after the 1918 Revolution, resulting in modern-day Cyrillic.

Greek

Greek writing goes back more than 2,700 years, and is one of the oldest scripts known. It evolved out of the Phoenician alphabet, with the addition of vowels to the original consonant script. The letters are constructed from basic geometric shapes such as the circle, square, and triangle, and their variations. It is a tribute to the Greeks' sense of proportion and formal sophistication. During the 9th century minuscules were beginning to be added to what had been a capital based script.

Many variations evolved from Greek script during its long history, such as Cyrillic and Etruscan, and right down to the Latin alphabet.

Hebrew

Modern Hebrew, the so-called square script, is derived from the oldest known Aramaic script, itself going back to Phoenician script. A system to denote vowels by means of dots was developed in the 9th century. Hebrew script contains 22 letters and is written from right to left. Another characteristic is its square-oblong formal appearance and its unconnected letters which remain unlinked even in their cursive form.

index of typefaces which are suitable for the screen

5.06

136.137

Non-Latin scripts |
Arabic
Devanagari

With their intricacy and rich, curvilinear detail Arabic
and Indian fonts have to be very carefully considered
for their suitability on screen.

»You wonder at beauty and behold flawless shape and figure,
I, however, can see nothing but artifice,
the art of the Creator and his beauty.«
Mohammed Dandamawaz Gisudaraz

Arabic

on screen | Akhbar

والخاء تحدث من ضغط الهواء إلى الحدا

والخاء تحدث من ضغط الهواء إلى الحدا

Andale Arabic

من ضغط الهواء إلى ا

Devanagari

on screen | ITC Chakra

हा निबंध हे अनेक वर्षे छपाईकलेच्या

हा निबंध हे अनेक वर्षे छपाईकलेच्या

Monotype Devanagari

हा निबंध हे अं

**Arabic
Devanagari**

Arabic script is predominantly curvilinear, and
visibly close to its calligraphic origin, even in its
printed form. Calligraphic skill in handwriting
which may be quite ornamental is considered
a great asset in Arabic culture (see left). Hence
Arabic scripts may often appear painterly (viz.
Arabesque).

Even simplified versions contain fine detail and
huge variations in boldness of stroke which are
hard to reproduce on screen. Fonts like Arabic
Web (see right) with bold and rather unified
strokes are designed to cope with these
drawbacks. Hook-like characters and detail are
appropriately sized.

With its plentiful curves and fine detail Indian
Devanagari script is similar to Arabic script.
Both are beautiful to look at but inappropriate
on screen. They are adaptable only in large sizes
and when placed in good contrast with coloured
backgrounds and other fonts.

Arabic Web

فير و شكا

From left to right:
Website with Arabic script
Website with Indian script

---

on screen | **Arabic Web**

ك ق ف غ ع ظ ظ ط ط ض ص ش س ز ر ذ د خ ح ج ج ث ت ب ا

١٢٣٤٥٦٧٨٩٠

With its curved lines and evidently calligraphic approach Arabic script is not well suited for reproduction on screen. When selecting fonts for the screen, typefaces such as Andale or Arab Web, with wide arches and unified boldness of stroke are preferable.

The Arabic letter »t«:
From right to left:
at the beginning,
in the middle,
and at the end of a word,
and as an individual,
separated letter.

نَ تَ ثَ تَ ت

---

on screen | **ITR Hari**
vanagari

हा निबंध हे अनेक वर्षे छपाईकलेच्या पाया

हा निबंध हे अनेक वर्षे छपाईकलेच्या पाया

In its intricacy Indian script is similarly inconvenient for reproduction on screen. Fonts should be carefully selected for their suitability on screen and applied in appropriate sizes. Use monotype, for instance.

ग्यारह बजे वहां पहुंचा था और पौने
सन्देश लाया हूं कि कमला अपनी भाभ
उसकी मां तो रजनी भाभी के घर पर श
HINDI

उल्लू वल वेखिआ दी ना जादे । उस नाल अँदे
पिछ-तूरदे तुरदे मोड़ीआं तें काराज
के धाएगा वो जा दंदिआ वदंगा ता दी मूह
GURMUKHI

Arabic

The origin of Arabic script with its 28 letters is found in ancient Nabatean. Like many Semitic scripts it is written from right to left which goes back to Phoenician tradition. Numbers are an exception as they are written from left to right. Thus Arabic is described as bi-directional.
There are other peculiarities in Arabic script which seem to be unusual for the European understanding: depending on their position within the text letters can have various shapes.

Characters are usually linked, there is no differentiation between capitals and minuscules. Arabic is consonant-based and diacritics are used to denote vowels only in the Koran and in poetry and longer literary works. With the wide dispersal of Islam, Arabic script is now prevalent in many countries. Frequently used scripts are Nashk (which permits vocalisation) in printing, Ruqaa in handwriting (no vowels), as well as Maghribi, Diwani, and Thuluth.

Devanagari

Devanagari goes back to the 11th century and has been used for a number of languages like Hindi, Marathi, Nepali, or Kashmiri, which in turn originate from Brahmi writing which has existed for nearly 2,000 years. With its long tradition, Indian script has undergone at least as many alterations and extensions as Latin scripts. In India, there are more than 10 officially recognised languages and more than twice that number of scripts.
Devanagari is written from left to right along a characteristic horizontal line. Formerly, sentences were separated by vertical lines, there were no separations between individual words. Today, Western punctuation has been adopted as separation marks.

How to design a
typeface suitable for
the screen

The maxim for suitable types for the screen could be:
bigger, wider, further.

▪▪▪▪▪▪▪

»A good type is not created by good intentions.«
Gui Bonsiepe

Verdana | Akzidenz Grotesk

Typography

Base line   x-height   x-height

**Fine lines do not reproduce
on screen. Recommended
are types consisting of bold
and uniform line.**

**Text includes mainly
minuscules. Increasing
the x-height of Verdana
improves legibility
on screen.**

Avantgarde   ao Il1   Gill Sans   ao Ill   Verdana   ao Il1

**1.2
From left to right:
minuscule »A«
minuscule »O«
capital »I«
minuscule »L«
digit »1«.**

**Immediate character
recognition is a prime
prerequisite for the design
of suitable type for screen
usage. The absence of serifs
in the more structural
geometric Grotesque types
makes them less conclu-**

**sive. In Verdana the capital
»i« with its solid serifs
appears out of order, but it
is clearly distinguishable
from the minuscule »i« or
the digit »1«.**

Types for the screen

The maxim for suitable types for the screen could
be: bigger, wider, further.
With today's standard pixel grid the appearance
of clumps can be prevented through generous
spacing between characters, as well as the application of large punch whites and elevated x-heights
to create an impression of size and lightness.

1.1   voluminous »o« in Verdana

Fine serifs and lines are not reproduced on screen
and should be omitted in favour of a uniform
graphic impression. Lines that are bolder than in
conventional typefaces are particularly well suited
for display on screen.
An important consideration for successful on-
screen display must be the shape of the characters

circular »o« in Avantgarde

(1.1): avoiding arches will improve the appearance
of characters on the orthogonal pixel grid of the
screen. Shapes should moreover be designed so as
to avoid any mistakes with similar characters, a
pitfall that easily occurs with poor reproduction

squared »o« in Eurostile

on standard low resolution screens (1.2). Stylistic
deviations such as with the capital I in Verdana
may seem unsophisticated but they do function
to aid distinctiveness.

oblong »o« in OCR A

The importance of an individual appearance
of a character should not be underestimated.
Designing a typeface only in accordance with the

requirements of the pixel grid will not yield the
expected results. The effect would be similar to
the geometric linear Antiquas. Their aesthetic
appeal is marred by the well-calculated geometric
structure of the characters, which gives them a
rather solitary appearance, to the detriment of
legibility.
Although the designer must consider the rigors
of the pixel grid he or she should also contem-
plate the individuality of characters and their
relation to one another.

Typography Typography

There are huge differences amongst certain types: look at the distinctions between **ITC Garamond and Adobe Garamond. Older types like Garamond have often been altered for today's require-** ments: in this case the example on the left has been given a more gener- ous width and bigger punch whites, as well as more elevated x-heights, than the example on the right, which is more traditional in appearance.

Verticals in a type designed for screen applications must not be smaller than 5 pt.
This can be illustrated by the relevant structure of a capital E: there are three horizontal strokes that must be kept apart on two respective vertical planes, making up a total mini- mum of 5 vertical pixels.

Such minimalist structures are only suitable for pixel fonts such as Mini 7, for captions and short texts in buttons or orientation.

1
2
3
4
5

Further remarks on the use of different types on screen

People from all over the world are given access via the Internet to diverse cultural backgrounds with their specific language and writing systems. Latin script occurs most commonly, mainly because the standardisation of computer operating systems evolved mainly in Europe and North America. The prevalence of Latin script represents a compromise which, at least, seems to be widely accepted.

Nevertheless the Western World has been ignorant of the co-existence of a huge number of other scripts that are extremely relevant in their respective regions. 4000 year-old traditions such as that of Chinese cannot simply be ignored. Could there be a universally adaptable and legible type for the Internet? It is soon obvious that other scripts, in comparison with Latin, are more suitably reproduced on screen. Korean or Hebrew characters slot more easily into the pixel grid, and Chinese characters are very economical in their use of space. For a universal script relevant specifics for each language would have to be included. Latin, for instance, makes no provision for the pronunciation of certain guttural sounds found in Arabic, and there are no vowels to resemble certain Vietnamese sounds.

transfer of corporate identity structures: **from print to screen**

Things to watch out for when transferring established typographical conventions to the screen.

From print to screen

Print and new media are very different. Therefore it is impossible to faithfully transfer a typographical presentation from one medium to another. There can only be an approximation of the original.

»With design being an inherently collaborative process the final product has always been a matter of contention.«
Zuzana Licko and Rudy VanderLans

Catalogue | digital

Welcome to the
Audi World Site

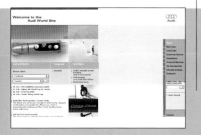

The use of the Audi Sans font (as a GIF-image) for captions to replicate familiar aspects from in-house print publications.

Verdana distinguishes other text.
The typeface Verdana can be read by all browsers and can be edited quickly.

ahlkarosserien gegen Perforation
wegen Vollverzinkung und Audi Space-F
2 Jahre Gewährleistung auf Audi Origina
Austausch Teile und Original Zubehör

Catalogue | print

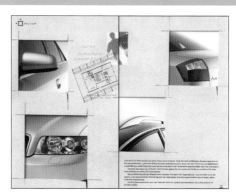

Same colour-mood on the Audi print publication and the website: Both media make use of the same metallic tones, as well as green and blue.

Transfer of corporate identity structures

Print media are usually published on a vertical format, whereas new media primarily appear on a horizontal format. Therefore it is impossible to transfer any typographical design from one to the other on a one-to-one basis. There are other factors to consider, too: the way that type looks on a computer screen depends on the various individual adjustments on each screen. It is therefore not really a fixed entity, like in print. Any typographical text design still has its limitations set by the drawbacks of standard low resolution screens. To overcome this predicament you may use specific features from the design which can be duplicated well on screen. These could be an image, a colour, or a logo that is also available in a suitable image file. The choice of type for general text should be confined to standard system fonts, which are easy to exchange and edit on any computer.

Often typography cannot be transferred from one medium to another. Recognition of corporate identity can be ensured through key familiar images or type fonts.

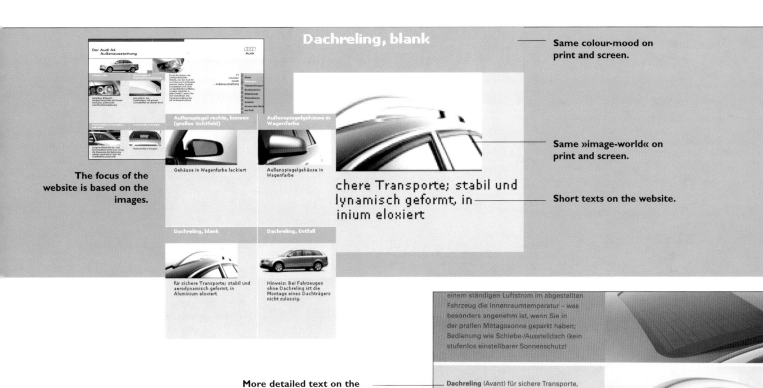

Same colour-mood on print and screen.

The focus of the website is based on the images.

Same »image-world« on print and screen.

Short texts on the website.

More detailed text on the print publication because type is more legible than on screen.

Audi Sans Extended Roman

Audi Sans Extended Italic

Audi Sans Extended Bold

Audi Sans Extended Bold Italic

Audi Sans Roman

Audi Sans Italic

Audi Sans Bold

Audi Sans Bold Italic

Typefaces for Audi Sans on screen.

Meta Design were commissioned to reshape the look of car manufacturer Audi's corporate identity. The task was to create a versatile typographic image suitable for anything from logo to general text content that would be adaptable for any medium.
An in-house type was offered as a solution. Audi Sans, derived from Univers, is available with various typefaces that are all equally suitable for either print or new media: all typefaces are very appropriate for screen display e.g. extended and bold. Note the absence of emphasis such as »condensed« and »thin« which were omitted on purpose.

Hans R. Bossard
Typografie, Schrift, Lesbarkeit
Niggli, Sulgen 1996

Cyrus Dominik Khazaelis
Crashkurs Typo and Layout.
Vom Schriftdesign zum visuellen Konzept
Rowohlt, Reinbek 2001

Joseph Müller-Brockmann
Rastersysteme für die visuelle Gestaltung
Niggli, Sulgen 1996

Veruschka Götz
Color & Type for the Screen
RotoVision, Hove 1996

Erik Spiekermann
Studentenfutter oder:
Was ich schon immer über Typografie wissen wollte,
mich aber nie zu fragen traute
Context GmbH, Nürnberg 1989

Jan Tschichold
Erfreuliche Drucksachen durch gute Typografie
Maro Verlag, Augsburg 2002

Rene Spitz
HfG Ulm, Der Blick hinter den Vordergrund
Herbert L. König, München 2002

Vittorio Magnago Lampugnani
Die Modernität des Dauerhaften
Wagenbach, Berlin 1995

Max Bill
Typographie, Reklame, Buchgestaltung
Niggli, Sulgen 1999

Otl Aicher
Typografie
Ernst & Sohn, Berlin 1988

Adrian Frutiger
Der Mensch und seine Zeichen
Fourier Verlag GmbH, Wiesbaden 1991

Ott | Stein | Friedl
Typografie
Könemann, Köln 1998

Harald Haarmann
Universalgeschichte der Schrift
Campus Verlag, Frankfurt/Main; New York 1991

Lewis Blackwell
20th century type | remix
Laurence King Publishing, London 1998

Veruschka Götz
Grids for the Internet and Other Digital Media
AVA Publishing SA, Worthing 2002

Ulli Neutzinger
Typo und Layout im Web
Rowohlt, Reinbek 2002

Molly E. Holzschlag
Farbe für Websites
Rowohlt, Reinbek 2001

Studio 7.5
Navigation for the Internet and Other Digital Media
AVA Publishing SA, Worthing 2002

MUTABOR | Robert Klanten
lingua grafica
Die Gestalten Verlag, Berlin 2001

Steven Heller | Philip B. Meggs
Texts on Type.
Critical Writings on Typography
Allworth Press, New York 2001

Jan Tschichold
The New Typography
University of California Press 1995

Eric Gill
An Essay on Typography
Dent, London 1936

Berthold-Schriftenbibliothek | Georg Salden
Das Stulle-Buch
zum Vergleichen, Auswählen, Erkennen und Finden
von Schriften
Stuttgart 1991

www.adobe.com/type

www.agfamonotype.com

www.digital-web.com

www.fontshop.com

www.microsoft.com/typography

www.stthomas.edu/webauthor

www.wpdfd.com/wpdtypo.html

http://info.med.yale.edu

The main text in this book is set in Gill Sans and the headlines and captions in Gill Sans Bold.

index

Many thanks to all the companies and design .... made their work available to me.

For their research and co-operation I would like to extend my thanks to:
**Alexander Fyjis-Walker, Reinald Gussmann,
Enno Hyttrek, Prof. Michael Klar and Wulf Beck, Bernhard Lassahn,
Stefanie Schlüter and Nicolas Taffin**

For their work and passion I would like to thank:
Anika Grebe, Andrea Jenzer and Martin Langer

And a very special thanks to Brian Morris, publisher of AVA Publishing SA,
to Natalia Price-Cabrera for her attention to detail and to Tessa Blakemore
for her kindness and support.

index